INDIA'S OLYMPIC MEDAL WINNERS

PARIS 1900 - PARIS 2024

INDIA'S OLYMPIC MEDAL WINNERS

PARIS 1900 - PARIS 2024

VIJAYAN BALA

PG PUBLICATION
Delhi -110089 (India)

Edition : First published 2024
ISBN : 978-93-6210-367-3

Price : 500/-

India's Olympic Medal Winners
Paris 1900 - Paris 2024
By : Vijayan Bala
Email Id : vijayanbala@hotmail.com

Cover Page & Book Layout
Jyoti Singh

Published by
PRAKHAR GOONJ PUBLICATION
Reg. Office: H-3/2, Sector-18, Rohini, Delhi-110089
Email : prakhargoonj@gmail.com
sinha.neelu123@gmail.com
Ph. : 7982710571, 7838505899, 011-42635077
Web : prakhargoonjpublications.com

About The Author

Mr Vijayan Bala is basically an educationist who has taught English in reputed schools such as Don Bosco (Park Circus), Kolkata, Modern School, Barakhamba Road, New Delhi and St. Xavier's Old Delhi, been Vice Principal at the Army Public School, Dhaula Kuan, New Delhi and finished off as Principal of Raunaq Public School, Ganaur near Sonepat. In the schools he has worked in, he was greatly involved in co-curricular and sports activities. He has also conducted workshops for English teachers in many reputed schools.

In the field of Sports, he has written freelance from the age of 18 for annual publications such as INDIAN CRICKET, magazines such as Sportsweek, Sportsworld, Weekend Review, Sun, Alive and Woman's Era and newspapers like Hindustan Times, The Hindu and The Telegraph. He has been on the statistical committees of the Board of Control for Cricket in India and the Cricket Association of Bengal. In 1974, he brought out INDIAN TEST CRICKET - A Statistical Digest which had a foreword by Mr Vijay Merchant. He has five other books to his credit - The Complete Indian Sports Quiz Book with a foreword by Olympic medallist Col Rajyavardhan Singh Rathore, two books containing his interviews with famous Indian sports personalities, ' On Being A Quality Educator' and Improving Your English Skills. In addition to this book - his seventh, another book of his on the Olympics for an international audience will be coming out soon. Mr Bala has been an English commentator for Akashvani and Doordarshan covering Cricket, Hockey and Football. He has also passed the state level umpiring exam conducted by the Delhi and Districts Cricket Association.

THE AUTHOR WITH INDIA'S SUCCESSFUL OLYMPIC STARS

Abhinav Bindra - India's first individual Olympic gold medallist. He was awarded the Olympic Order by the IOC in 2024.

Neeraj Chopra - India's second individual Olympic gold medallist. He is the first Indian to win a gold and a silver in successive Olympics.

Manu Bhaker - The first Indian woman to win two medals in a single Olympic Games.

ABHINAV A. BINDRA

2nd May, 2024

Foreword

It gives me great pleasure in writing the foreword for Mr Vijayan Bala's new book on India's Olympic medal winners. I have gone through Mr Bala's earlier works - a quiz book on Indian Sports and two collections of 77 interviews each of well-known Indian sports personalities and found that they not only contained a wealth of information but were also very interesting to read.

India's medals in the Olympics have come in the men's Field Hockey event and in a few other sporting events. In this well-researched book, Mr Bala not only enables readers to know through his write-ups and interviews about the achievements and struggles of all our individual medal winners and prominent hockey stars but also how they brought glory for India and themselves.

The incidents and stories in this book must be known and cherished by every Indian be it through libraries, institutions and bookshops. I wish Mr Bala all the best and sincerely hope that everyone picks up a copy of the book which I feel will inspire many others to take up sport, support Indian sports persons and breed a culture of Sporting Excellence in India!

Abhinav Bindra

PREFACE

My book on "India's Olympic Medal Winners" deals with India's Olympic medal winners from the 1900 till the 2024 Olympics. The purpose of this book is to inform, educate and inspire readers. The book contains interviews of our individual medal winners in different sports wherein we are told about how they won their medals. Descriptions of how Indian hockey teams won their medals along with interviews and write-ups of some of our hockey greats and captains of those teams also feature in the book. The book also contains pictures of our individual medal winners, hockey captains and medal-winning hockey teams. I wish to thank the different sources for the photographs. For the identification of the members of the Indian hockey teams from 1948 till 1968, I am grateful to Mr. Gurbux Singh, a former Indian Olympic hockey captain.

After going through the manuscript, the late Mr. Balbir Singh (Sr.) had this to say, "I strongly recommend this book to be read by the younger generation in particular. Who knows, learning from such stories might help them -one day to make another mark on the world map not only in sports but in any field of their choice. I congratulate Vijayan for giving practical shape to my thoughts that can guide and encourage millions of Indians to take up Sports!"

Finally, I wish to express my gratitude to the late Mr. Balbir Singh (Sr.) for his words of appreciation and Mr. Abhinav Bindra for kindly consenting to write the foreword.

Bala

(Vijayan Bala)

CONTENTS

CHAPTER 1

1900 PARIS GAMES - INDIA'S FIRST OLYMPIC MEDAL

The general impression among sports enthusiasts is that India's first Olympic medal was won by the men's hockey team which got the gold medal in the 1928 Amsterdam Olympics. However, the truth is India's first Olympic medal was won by Norman Pritchard, an Indian athlete of English origin in the 1900 Paris Olympics.

In the Paris Games, the track and field events took place on an uneven field of grass littered with trees. Pritchard was the first and only Indian participant in the 1900 Olympics. He won two silver medals. Norman Pritchard won his first silver medal on 16th July 1900 when he finished second to Alvin Kraenzlein in the men's 200m hurdles event. Six days later on 22nd July, Pritchard won his second Olympic silver medal when he finished second to Walter Tewksbury in the men's 200m event. Norman Pritchard also competed in the 110m hurdles event without success. He could not qualify for the finals of the 60m and 100m race events. Tewksbury won five medals including two golds while Kraenzlein finished with four individual gold medals in that Olympics. Both Kraenzlein and Tewksbury were from Pennsylvania University training to be dentists.

Before the 1900 Olympics, Norman visited England with his father for business. It was on that trip he participated in the English athletics circuit. In the British Athletics Championships (AAA Championships), he performed well while representing Bengal Presidency Athletic Club. This performance reportedly helped him achieve qualification for the 1900 Paris Olympics. He was referred to as an 'Indian Champion' by The Field magazine.

There has been controversy about whether Pritchard was representing India or Britain in the Paris Olympics, and both countries have claimed the medals to be attributed to their Olympic hauls. The International Olympic Committee's official website mentions Pritchard as having represented India and the two medals are counted in India's tally. The athlete's association with Bengal Presidency Athletic Club (while participating in the AAA Championships) is reported to be a reason for Pritchard being considered as a participant from British India. The IOC still regards Pritchard as having competed for India, and his two medals are credited to India.

Norman Pritchard was born on 23rd June 1877 at Calcutta (now Kolkata), West Bengal to George Peterson Pritchard and Helen Maynard Pritchard. George was an accountant, settled at Alipore, Calcutta. Norman studied at St. Xavier's College, Calcutta and used to play football for his college. He is said to have been the first Indian to score a hat-trick in an Open Football Tournament in India, which he did in a match for St. Xavier's College against Sovabazar in the year 1897. He also initially worked at Bird & Co. in Kolkata.

As an athlete the best performance by Norman in India was delivered in a 100 yards race on grass in Calcutta (Kolkata) on 18th February 1898. Although no official world records were maintained those days, Norman's timing of 9.8 seconds is said to be equal to the same delivered by world class sprinters of the time. From the year 1894 to 1900, he won the Bengal Province 100 yards sprint title, the 440 yards and 120 yards hurdles races. Between the years 1900 and 1902, Norman served as the Secretary of the Indian Football

Association, and permanently moved to England in the year 1905 to trade in jute.

After his relocation to England, Norman was invited by Sir Charles Wyndham, a theatre personality to perform a role in his play, 'The Stronger Sex', in the year 1907. After the play proved to be a great success, Sir Charles advised him to move to the USA and take up acting seriously. Following his suggestion, Norman made his debut at Broadway in the USA with the play 'The Elder Son' in the year 1914. The next year he made his silent movie debut with a movie named 'After Dark'. He acted in 26 plays and 27 movies. His last movie 'Tonight at Twelve' was released in the year 1929.

Norman Pritchard had many firsts to his name - he was the first Indian and the first Asian to win Olympic medals, he was also the first Olympian to act on the stage in England and on the big screen in silent Hollywood movies under the screen name, Norman Trevor.

Norman Pritchard had a very sad end as he died of a mental disease called brain malady at Norwalk, California on 31st October 1929.

Pritchard may have been of English heritage but he was born in India, grew up there and learnt the sport and later spent some time as an administrator as well in the country. He proved to everyone that it was possible for athletes coming from Asia to compete with the best in the world.

CHAPTER 2

INDIA'S FIRST HOCKEY GOLD – 1928 AMSTERDAM OLYMPICS

India competed at the 1928 Amsterdam Olympics in three sports – Hockey, Athletics and Swimming. The men's field hockey team won the gold medal for the first time in the Olympics while our seven athletes and one swimmer were unsuccessful in their efforts. Jaipal Singh Munda was the official captain of the Indian hockey side.

Jaipal Singh Munda was a politician, prolific writer and sportsman. He was the member of the Constituent Assembly which debated on the new Constitution of the Indian Union. Later, he emerged as a campaigner for the cause of Adivasis and the creation of a separate homeland for them in central India. As a member of the Constituent Assembly of India, he campaigned for the rights of the whole tribal community.

Jaipal Singh Munda, also known as Pramod Pahan, was born in a Munda tribal family, on 3rd January 1903 in Takra, Pahan Toli village of what was then Khunti subdivision (now declared district) of the then district of Ranchi in the Bihar Province of British India (in the present-day state of Jharkhand). In childhood, Jaipal's job was to look after cattle. After initial schooling at the village church school, in 1910 he gained admission to St. Paul's College, Ranchi, which was run by the Christian Missionaries of the SPG Mission of the Church of England. A gifted field hockey player, Jaipal was a brilliant student who exhibited exceptional leadership qualities from a very young age. This was noticed by the missionaries, who took him to England for higher studies at the University of Oxford. He graduated from St. John's College, Oxford with Honours in Economics.

Jaipal was selected to work in the Indian Civil Service, from which he later resigned. In 1934, he became a teacher at the Prince of Wales College at Achimota, Gold Coast, Ghana. In 1937, he returned to India as the Principal of the Rajkumar College, Raipur. In 1938, he joined the Bikaner princely state as foreign secretary. The same year, he decided to enter politics after seeing the poor condition of the tribal people.

Jaipal was a member of the Oxford University hockey team. The hallmarks of his game as a deep defender were his clean tackling, sensible gameplay and well-directed hard hits. He was the most versatile player in the Oxford University hockey team. His contribution to the University hockey team was recognised and he became the first Indian student to be conferred a Blue in hockey.

In 1928, while he was in England, Jaipal was asked to captain the Indian hockey team for the 1928 Olympic Games. Jaipal was a household name in English hockey circles. His intimate knowledge of English ground conditions proved very helpful. Due to a dispute with the Englishman team manager, A. B. Rossier, Jaipal left the team after the semi-final and so he did not play the final. In the final, the Indian team defeated the Netherlands 3-0.

On returning to India, Jaipal was associated with Mohun Bagan Club of Calcutta and started its hockey team in 1929. He led that team in various tournaments. After retirement from active hockey, he served as Secretary of the Bengal Hockey Association and as a member of the Indian Sports Council.

Jaipal died of cerebral hemorrhage on 20th March 1970 at his residence in New Delhi. He was 68 and left behind four children — a daughter and three sons. A stadium named after him was opened in Ranchi in 2013.

Above: ***The All India hockey team which won the Olympic title. 8 of the playing 11 members were Anglo-Indians and, of the two reserves, one was an Anglo-Indian.***

Indian Team : Jaipal Singh Munda (Captain), Broome Eric Pinniger (Captain in the final), Richard Allen, Dhyan Chand, Maurice Gately, William Goodsir-Cullen, Leslie Hammond, Feroze Khan, S.M. Yusuf, George Marthins, Rex Norris, Michael Rocque, Frederic Seaman, Shaukat Ali and Kher Singh Gill.

India, the Netherlands, Germany, Belgium, Austria, Denmark, France, Switzerland and Spain were the nine countries that participated in the hockey event of the 1928 Olympics. The teams were divided into two groups. India was in Group A. The winners of the groups played the final for the gold and silver medals. The runners-up of the groups played for the bronze medal.

On 17th May, India easily defeated Austria 6-0 in its opening fixture played in fine weather conditions. The following day, India scored a 9-0 win over Belgium. In the next match on 20th May, India, despite facing a defiant goal-keeper, scored a 5-0 win over Denmark. In the last group match on 22nd May, India outclassed Switzerland 6-0 to top the group.

In the final on 26th May, the Indian side were without the injured Feroze Khan, the ill Shaukat Ali and Jaipal Singh who had left the team after the semi-final. According to some reports, Jaipal was distraught with the lack of support from the nine (eight in the first eleven) Anglo-Indian members within the team. Pinniger led India in Jaipal's absence. Despite these issues, India won the summit clash by a 3-0 margin with Dhyan Chand despite being very ill scoring yet another hat-trick. The Netherlands fought gallantly in the final. They raised their game being supported by a cheering crowd of 50, 000. India became Olympic champions.

The 1928 Amsterdam Olympics where India won the hockey gold for the first time in the Olympics saw the birth of a legend in Dhyan Chand who was the top scorer of the tournament with 14 goals, including a hat-trick in the final against the Netherlands. India scored 29 goals and did not concede a single goal in five matches. Richard Allen was the goalkeeper. India's performance was greatly praised and while only three persons saw them off on their journey to London on 10th March 1928 by ship 'Kaiser-i-Hind', massive crowds thronged the Bombay port to welcome the new Olympic champions.

Results:

League - beat Austria 6-0 (Dhyan Chand 3, George Marthins 2, Shaukat All 1)

beat Belgium 9-0 (Feroze Khan 5, Frederic Seaman 2, George Marthins 1, Dhyan Chand 1)

beat Denmark 5-0 (Dhyan Chand 3, Frederic Seaman 1, George Marthins 1)

beat Switzerland 6-0 (Dhyan Chand 4, Maurice Gately 1, George Marthins 1).

Final - beat the Netherlands 3-0 (Dhyan Chand 3)

Final Positions - India 1, the Netherlands 2, Germany 3, Belgium 4, Spain 5, France 6, Denmark 7, Austria 8, Switzerland 9.

CHAPTER 3

HOCKEY GOLD AGAIN IN 1932 LOS ANGELES OLYMPICS

Four years later at the 1932 Los Angeles Olympics, India again participated in Hockey, Athletics and Swimming. India once again won the hockey gold. There was a paucity of entries for the hockey event. Pankaj Gupta, an influential Indian sports administrator, prevailed upon Japan to take part to make it the minimum three teams required for the competition. USA, the hosts, was the other nation in addition to India. Hockey was the only event in which India won a medal. Syed Lal Shah Bokhari captained the Indian side.

Syed Lal Shah Bokhari, was born in Faisalabad on 22nd July 1909. He migrated to Pakistan upon Pakistan's independence. He was a Punjab Civil Serviceman and at the time of partition he was President of the Delhi Hockey Association. He served as a diplomat for Pakistan – his last posting was Pakistan High Commissioner in Ceylon (Sri Lanka) where he died on 22nd July 1959.

He was a good half-back who was controversially selected skipper of the team ahead of Broome Eric Pinniger – then the best centre-half in the world and captain of India in the final of the 1928 Olympics. His selection as captain brought about groupism (Indians vs Anglo Indians) in the side which had seven Anglo Indians. However, according to the great Dhyan Chand, a member of the side, Bokhari was a grand team-man and a great leader. He was also an excellent athlete and established several records in the Punjab. **He was India's flag-bearer at the Opening Ceremony.**

Indian Team: Syed Lal Shah Bokhari (Captain), Richard J. Allen, Arthur Charles Hind, Mohammed Aslam, Carlyle Carrol Tapsell, Leslie Charles Hammond, Masud Ali Khan Minhas, Broome Eric Pinniger, Frank Brewin, Richard John Carr, Gurmit Singh Kullar, Dhyan Chand, Roop Singh, Syed Mohammed Jaffar and William Sullivan.

A number of officials are also seen above.

The Indian side won both their matches in the 1932 Olympics. Despite scoring 35 goals, the Indian side conceded a goal in both the games. In the 1928 Olympics, the Indian side did not concede a single goal.

Dhyan Chand and Roop Singh.

On 4th August, India defeated Japan 11-1 in its first match. The goal which goalkeeper Allen conceded was the first goal he had conceded in the Olympics. In that game, India took Japan lightly as they had met Japan on the way to the United States and so knew the strength of the Japanese side. However, the Japanese side played much better during the Games. The only goal Japan scored was in the second half when they were down

0-4. The goal was scored by Inochora, their left-winger who converted a penalty corner with a quick flick that entered the net between the goalkeeper Allen and full-back Tapsell.

On 11th August, India met United States of America in the deciding match of the tournament. India scored an easy 24-1 win. The funny part of the goal India conceded was that it was a result of India's goalkeeper Richard Allen being busy signing autographs for fans. Certain American newspapers had suggested that in order to make the game a contest, the Indians ought to play left-handed or wear snow shoes. At half-time, India was leading 10-0. India's main goal scorers in the two matches were Roop Singh, the younger brother of Dhyan Chand (13 goals), Dhyan Chand (12 goals) and Gurmit Singh Kullar (8 goals).

Results:

beat Japan 11-1 (Dhyan Chand 4, Roop Singh 3, Gurmit Singh Kullar 3 and Richard Carr 1)

beat USA 24-1 (Roop Singh 10, Dhyan Chand 8, Gurmit Singh Kullar 5 and Broome Eric Pinniger 1)

Final Positions - India 1, Japan 2, USA 3.

CHAPTER 4

HAT-TRICK OF OLYMPIC HOCKEY GOLDS - 1936 BERLIN

The Indian hockey side under the captaincy of the great Dhyan Chand completed a hat-trick of golds in the Olympic hockey event in the 1936 Berlin Olympics. Dhyan Chand also won his third successive Olympic hockey gold. India also participated in Athletics and Freestyle Wrestling.

All the matches took place either in the Hockey Stadium or on the Hockey Stadium Field No.2. Both the field hockey grounds were near the Olympic Stadium located on the Reichssportfeld. The competition was held from 4th August to 15th August. Eleven teams which were divided in three groups participated. India was in Group A. The field hockey matches saw a total attendance of 1, 84, 103 and 1, 57, 531 tickets were sold. The Indian team scored 38 goals and conceded one.

The Berlin Games was to be Dhyan Chand's third and last Olympics at the age of 31, for he had decided to retire. **He was India's flag-bearer at the Opening Ceremony.** Undoubtedly at the peak of his prowess, he was handed the Indian team's captaincy and this time, there was no dissent, though the omission of Richard Carr raised a few eyebrows. Carr was not released by the Indian Railways. The run-up to the Games was not exactly satisfactory. A 1-4 defeat to Germany in a practice game rang alarm bells in the Indian camp. Following a team meeting, it was decided to bring in Ali Iqtidar Shah Dara who was to represent Pakistan in the 1948 Olympics following partition.

Indian Team: Dhyan Chand (Captain), Syed Mohammed Jaffar, lqtidar Ali Shah Dara, Richard James Allen, Mohammed Hussain, Ahmed Sher Khan, Carlyle Carrol Tapsell, Baboo Narsoo Nimal, Ernest John Goodsir-Cullen, Ashan Mohammed Khan, Joseph Gallibardy, Roop Singh, Gurcharan Singh Garewal, Lionel C Emmet, Mirza Nasir-ud-Din Masud, Paul Peter Fernandes, Joseph Phillips, Shabban Shaahab-ud-Din and Cyril Michie.

Seated 3rd from the left - Mr. Pankaj Gupta and 3rd from the right - Prof. Jagannath. (Both were officials)

On 5th August, India played its first match against Hungary. India could only win 4-0 because of the sound Hungarian defence and a plucky display by their goalkeeper. The ground having become heavy due to rain made things more difficult for the Indian side. Two days later, India beat USA 7-0 in ideal weather and ground conditions. USA did not put up much of a fight. India's next league match on 10th August was against Japan. India won 9-0 but for the first 20 minutes the score was 0-0 because Japan played stolidly having picked up a lot of Indian tactics. Dara reinforced the Indian side in the semi-final against France on 12th August. India scored an easy 10-0 win. Dara in his first appearance scored twice.

The final against hosts Germany was fixed for 14th August but due to heavy rains it was postponed to 11 a.m. the following day. A crowd of 40, 000 packed the hockey stadium. The defeat at the hands of Germany in a practice match prior to the Olympics made the Indian team nervous. In addition to playing the Indian brand of hockey, the Germans also undercut and lifted the ball but the Indian team countered these tactics with brilliant half-volleying and amazing long shots. At half-time, India led 1-0. In the second-half, Dhyan Chand discarded his spiked shoes and stockings and played bare feet. He moved more quickly after that. During the game, Dhyan Chand lost a tooth in a collision with the aggressive German goalkeeper. Returning to the field after medical attention, Dhyan Chand reportedly told his players to "teach a lesson" to the Germans by not scoring. The Indians repeatedly took the ball to the German circle only to back-pedal. After half-time, India put pressure and were 4-0 ahead when Germany scored through Weiss off a rebound from goalkeeper Allen's pads. That was the only goal India conceded in the tournament. India scored four more goals to win 8-1 and take the Olympic hockey gold medal for the third successive time.

Results:

League - beat Hungary 4-0 (Roop Singh 2, Carlyle Tapsell 1, Shabban Shaahab-ud-Din 1).

beat USA 7-0 (Syed Mohammed Jaffar 2, Dhyan Chand 2, Roop Singh 2, Ernest Goodsir-Cullen 1).

beat Japan 9-0 (Dhyan Chand 4, Peter Fernandes 2, Carlyle Tapsell 2, Roop Singh 1).

Semi-final - beat France 10-0 (Dhyan Chand 4, Roop Singh 2, Iqtidar Ali Dara 2, Carlyle Tapsell 1, Shabban Shaahab-ud-Din 1)

Final- beat Germany 8-1 (Dhyan Chand 3, Iqtidar Ali Dara 2, Roop Singh 1, Carlyle Tapsell 1, Syed Mohammed Jaffar 1).

Final Positions - India 1, Germany 2, the Netherlands 3, France 4, Switzerland 5, Afghanistan 6, Japan 7, Hungary 8, Belgium 9, Denmark 10, USA 11.

Dhyan Chand – The Hockey Maestro

The hockey legend Dhyan Singh was born on 29th August 1905 in Allahabad to Sharadha Singh and Sameshwar Singh – a soldier in the British Indian Army. A young Dhyan had no serious interest in sports, though he loved wrestling. Apart from an occasional game with his friends in Jhansi, Dhyan did not play any hockey worth mentioning before he joined the army. Dhyan Singh joined the Indian Army at the age of 16, in 1922. It was there that Dhyan Singh got his famous second name 'Chand' – as he used to train in the moonlight due to lack of floodlights and his army duty. In the army, his dribbling skills were noticed by Subedar-Major Bale Tiwari. Tiwari became his mentor and helped Dhyan Chand improve his game. Between 1922 and 1926, he played the army hockey tournaments and the regimental games. Eventually, Dhyan Chand was selected for the Indian Army team's tour of New Zealand.

The Indian side was firing on all cylinders in New Zealand, where they won 18 matches, drew two and just lost a solitary tie. Their performance was lauded by many and Dhyan Chand in particular received a lot of praise for his displays on his first international assignment. On return, he was named a Lance Naik in the Punjab Regiment of the British Indian Army. His quality and performance did not go unnoticed for long as Dhyan Chand would soon make it to the Indian team for the 1928 Amsterdam Olympics.

His splendid performance at the inter-provincial tournament as the centre-forward and his partnership with George Marthins, the inside-right, meant Dhyan Chand was in India's first-ever hockey squad for the Olympic Games.

Though they had to face some financial troubles before reaching Amsterdam, once in the Dutch city, the Indian team was in their groove as they made the competition their own with some fantastic hockey. Leading the charge was their centre-forward, Dhyan Chand, who top-scored with 14 goals in his five matches en route to a gold medal in their debut appearance.

The coming years would see Dhyan Chand's stature grow manifold as the man from Allahabad took his game a notch higher and helped India defend their Olympic gold at the 1932 Los Angeles Games. The win was a little more special as Dhyan had his brother Roop Singh along in the team that took the gold in Los Angeles.

While the previous two editions saw Dhyan Chand lead the Indian team with his emphatic performances on the field, at the 1936 Olympics in Berlin, he was named the skipper of the side. The added responsibility only spurred him to greater exploits. The Indian team scored a total of 38 goals in the competition as they bagged another Olympic gold conceding just one goal in the final. Dhyan Chand retired from international hockey in 1936 at the age of 31.

In 1956, at the age of 51, he retired from the army with the rank of Major. After he retired, he coached for a while and eventually settled in Jhansi. The last days of Dhyan Chand's life were not very happy as he was short of money and was badly ignored by the nation. Once, he went to a tournament in Ahmedabad and they turned him away not knowing who he was. He developed liver cancer and was sent to a general ward at the AIIMS, New Delhi. He was later shifted to a special ward as the news was highlighted in the press. He died on 3rd December 1979 in New Delhi. In 1956, Dhyan Chand was conferred the Padma Bhushan. His birthday is celebrated every year as National Sports Day. The Indian Postal Service issued a postage stamp in his memory and the National Stadium in New Delhi was named after him in 2002. In 2014, despite being a nominee for the Bharat Ratna, the powers that be decided to confer it on Sachin Tendulkar and C.N.R. Rao.

It is worth mentioning that his younger brother Roop Singh was also a member of the 1932 and 1936 gold medal winning Olympic hockey sides. In the 1932 Olympics, Dhyan Chand and Roop Singh scored 25 of the 35 goals India scored while in the 1936 Olympics the two brothers scored 21 off India's 38 goals. Roop Singh scored 21 goals in both the Olympics while Dhyan Chand, the master, scored 39 goals in the three Olympics he participated in.

Again, one of Dhyan Chand's sons – Ashok, also played for India with distinction in the 1970s. Ashok was a brilliant inside forward who scored India's winning goal against Pakistan in the final of the 1975 World Cup tournament in Kuala Lumpur. He is also an Olympic hockey bronze medallist in the 1972 Munich Olympics.

Some Interesting Incidents In Dhyan Chand's Life And Hockey Career

1. Once, when Dhyan Chand was unable to score in a match, he argued with the umpire about the measurement of the goalpost. To everybody's amazement, he was right, the goalpost was found to be in contravention of the official minimum width prescribed under international rules.

2. One journalist reported: 'It looks like he has some invisible magnet stuck to his hockey stick so that the ball does not leave it at all.' It did not end there. Hockey authorities in the Netherlands once broke his hockey stick to check if there was a magnet inside!

3. Australian cricketing great Don Bradman met Dhyan Chand at Adelaide in 1935. After watching him play, Bradman remarked, "He scores goals like runs in cricket".

4. After India's first match at the 1936 Berlin Olympics, people watching other sporting events thronged to the hockey stadium. A German newspaper carried a banner headline: 'The Olympic complex now has a magic show too.' The whole city of Berlin had posters: "Visit the hockey stadium to watch the Indian magician Dhyan Chand in action."

5. When India defeated Germany 8-1 in the hockey final of the 1936 Berlin Olympics, Hitler could not bear the humiliation and left before the game ended. According

to authentic reports, Hitler later offered to elevate 'Lance Naik' Dhyan Chand to the rank of an officer if he migrated to Germany. Dhyan Chand politely refused the offer.

6. To honour Dhyan Chand, the residents of Vienna, Austria had set up a statue with four hands and four hockey sticks, depicting his mastery in the game – his incredible hockey skills.

CHAPTER 5

INDEPENDENT INDIA WINS ITS FIRST HOCKEY GOLD IN 1948 LONDON OLYMPICS

It was a big achievement that India managed to field a hockey team for the 1948 London Olympics which was held on the conclusion of World War II and a year or so after the traumatic partition that threw the sub-continent into great turmoil. A hockey Olympic gold medal for independent India brought back smiles on the faces of Indians who were struggling to rebuild their lives in the aftermath of the partition.

The Indian Hockey Federation (IHF) with Naval Tata as its President, put together a team that represented a new generation of players, all of whom were set to make their Olympic debut, and some destined for greatness. **Kishan Lal of the Railways led the Indian hockey side.** India and Pakistan decided to field separate squads. The Indian contingent with 78 participants competed in 10 sports. **India's flag-bearer at the Opening Ceremony was the football captain Dr. T Ao.**

Kishan Lal was born in Mhow on 2nd February 1917. As a little child he was fascinated by the game polo which he used to often watch longingly. It triggered the player in him and soon he won the admiration of the crowds when he started playing hockey at the age of 14. In 1933, at the age of 16, he represented Mhow Heroes, Mhow Green Walls and also went on to play for Kalyanmal

Mills, Indore. He played along with Dhyan Chand for Jhansi Heroes. In 1937, his talent caught the eye of M. N. Zutshi - the captain of Bhagwant Club hockey team. Zutshi brought Kishan Lal's talent to the attention of the Maharaja of the erstwhile Tikamgarh State and thereafter Kishan Lal was seen donning the colours of the prestigious Bhagwant Club of Tikamgarh.

Kishan Lal was selected for the 1940 Olympic team but due to World War II, the Olympic Games of 1940 and 1944 were cancelled. In the year 1941, he joined the then BB & CI Railway now known as Western Railway. He played for Central India in the National Hockey Championship. He continued to figure prominently in the winning teams at the Aga Khan Cup, Beighton Cup, Obaidullah Khan Cup and the Scindia Cup tournaments. Under his captaincy, the team was victorious.

In 1947, he wore the Indian colours and was vice-captain to Dhyan Chand on a tour of East Africa. The following year he earned the honour of captaining the Indian team to the Olympic Games at London. This particular Olympic Games was very important to the country. India had just got her independence from the British after a very long and demanding struggle. The 1948 Olympics was being held in London itself and India had been partitioned to carve out Pakistan on account of which many talented players had migrated to Pakistan. The Indian team for the London Games was a new team without a single player with previous experience of the Olympics. However, this team led by Kishan Lal brought glory to India by beating Great Britain 4-0 in the final in its own backyard. It was a moment India will never forget. This victory brought great honour to the country because India had for the first time participated in these Games as an independent nation and for the first time, the Indian tri-colour was unfurled in the Olympic arena and the National Anthem 'Jana, Gana, Mana' was played.

Kishan Lal was one of the greatest right-wingers of his time. As a right-winger he was very intelligent. Though he was not very speedy, he had the wonderful ability to spot the other forwards and release the ball accurately and at the right moment to them so that they could score. Most important of all, he was a thorough gentleman.

After 28 years of active playing, Kishan Lal retired from competitive hockey but remained connected with the game till 1976 as chief coach under the Railways Sports Control Board. Players like Prithipal Singh, Mohinder Lal, Balbir Singh and Harbinder Singh owe their stature in a big way to his grooming. His talent spotting was admired greatly. In 1964, he was invited to train Malaysia. In 1968, he was invited to coach East Germany. Even after retiring from Western Railway in 1976, he displayed great interest in the Railway team and in the game. He was probably the only former Olympian who was a regular at hockey competitions.

In 1966, Kishan Lal was conferred the Padma Shri. He died in Madras (Chennai) on 23rd June 1980.

Indian Team: Standing (L to R) Jaswant Singh Rajput, R.S. Gentle, Amir Kumar, Tarlochan Singh Bawa, K. D. Singh 'Babu', Kishan Lal (Captain), Grahanandan (Nandy) Singh, Keshav Datt, Walter D'Souza, Gerald Glacken, R. Francis.

Kneeling (L to R) Leslie Claudius, Balbir Singh, Maxie Vaz, Lawrie Fernandes, Leo Pinto, Latif-ur-Rehman, Patrick Jansen. *Grahandan (Nandy) Singh was a late replacement for Reginald Rodrigues.*

In the London Olympics, the 13 participating teams were divided into three groups. India was in Group A. In its first match on 31st July, India scored an easy 8-0 win over Austria. In India's second game against Argentina on 4th August, Balbir Singh made his Olympic hockey debut when he was selected in place of the unwell Reginald Rodrigues. Balbir helped India win 9-1 by scoring six goals which included a hat-trick. However, for reasons best known to the team management, Balbir was not played against Spain in the quarter-final and the Netherlands in the semi-final. His absence was greatly felt as India struggled to beat Spain 2-0 on 6th August and the Netherlands 2-1 on 9th August. Balbir's replacements Grahanandan (Nandy) Singh and Gerald Glacken were no match for the wily centre-forward who was brought back for the final against Great Britain following an uproar.

In the final on 12th August, the British were a completely changed people. As the match started, they rent the air with shouts of "Come on Great Britain." This chant gave way to cheering Indians once India established its supremacy and the spectators knew the likely outcome. Twice during the match, a slight drizzle made the ground heavy and slippery. Kishan Lal and K.D. Singh 'Babu' took off their shoes and played barefoot. Great Britain was full of confidence for it had beaten the new nation Pakistan squarely in the semi-finals 2-0. However, the home team's confidence was short-lived as in the first half, Balbir scored twice - both hits taken from the top of the circle off passes from Kishan Lal and K.D. Singh 'Babu'. The spectators were thrilled. Tarlochan Singh converted a penalty corner early in the second half and Pat Jansen scored a field goal to end

British hopes. India won 4-0. The gold medal was won by independent India.

When I asked **Keshav Datt, a member of the side and a great half-back** about independent India's win in the hockey event, he said, "The 1948 hockey Olympic gold medal had the greatest significance for me and the team as it stood as a symbolic victory against the British who had ruled our country for many years."

Results:

League - beat Austria 8-0 (Kunwar Digvijay Singh 'Babu' 2, Patrick Jansen 4, Kishan Lal 1, Reginald Rodrigues 1).

beat Argentina 9-1 (Balbir Singh Dosanjh 6, Patrick Jansen 2, Kishan Lal 1).

Quarter-final - beat Spain 2-0 (Tarlochan Singh 1, Kunwar Digvijay Singh 'Babu' 1).

Semi-final - beat the Netherlands 2-1 (Gerald Glacken 1, Kunwar Digvijay Singh 'Babu' 1).

Final - beat Great Britain 4-0 (Balbir Singh Dosanjh 2, Tarlochan Singh 1, Patrick Jansen 1)

Final Positions - India 1, Great Britain 2, the Netherlands 3, Pakistan 4, Argentina 5, Switzerland 6, Belgium 7, Austria 8, Afghanistan 9, France 10, Spain 11, USA 12, Denmark 13.

CHAPTER 6

TWO MEDALS FOR INDIA IN THE 1952 HELSINKI OLYMPICS

For the second time since 1900, India won two medals in the Olympics. The Indian contingent comprising of 64 participants in 11 sports won a bronze medal in wrestling -K D Jadhav and a gold medal in men's hockey. Let me start with K D Jadhav.

Khashaba Dadasaheb Jadhav was India's first Olympic medal winner in Wrestling. Jadhav's journey to the 1952 Helsinki Olympics was far from a smooth ride, but he went on to make India proud by winning a bronze medal in Wrestling (Bantamweight category).

Jadhav was born on 15th January 1926 in Satara to a Maharashtrian family which was involved in wrestling. His father Dadasaheb, also a wrestler, noticed the potential Jadhav had. So he introduced him to the sport at the tender age of five. The rising wrestling champion hardly let anybody take him down despite having a non-sturdy build. He attended Tilak High School in Karad, a couple of kilometres from his village for primary education.

In 1948, while studying at Kolhapur's Raja Ram College, Jadhav approached his Principal seeking permission to participate in the annual sports meet after his sports teacher rejected him because of his physique. When finally allowed, his game stunned many as he knocked down the bulkiest of players. During his initial training years, before he went on to represent India at the 1948 and 1952 Olympic Games, Jadhav was trained by wrestlers Baburao Balawde and Belapuri Guruji.

In the 1948 Summer Olympics held in London, Jadhav did not win a medal but he impressed spectators in those matches where he defeated his opponents within minutes. Finishing sixth in the freeweight category was a major feat for an athlete who had just got the first taste of playing a match on the professional mat. The 1948 Games set the tone for Jadhav for the next Olympics in Helsinki, Finland, as he was more determined to win a medal for his country.

Jadhav had to fight rival Niranjan Das more than twice to be able to represent his country at the 1952 Helsinki Olympic Games. It is believed that it was at the behest of the Maharaja of Patiala, after Jadhav wrote to him, that a third bout was organised between Jadhav and Das. Jadhav knocked Das down yet again and was chosen to participate at the 1952 Olympics. But Jadhav still lacked finances to fund his stay there. His college's principal arranged a sum of Rs 7, 000 as he mortgaged his own house. Other people too contributed and took care of other requirements.

At Helsinki, during the wrestling event which was held from 20th to 23rd July, Jadhav astonished everybody with his easy wins over Adrien Poliquin of Canada in round 1, Leonardo Basurto of Mexico in round 2 and Ferdinand Schmitz of Germany in round 3, in the freestyle bantamweight category. Jadhav got a bye in round 4, In round 5, Soviet Union's Rashid Mammadbeyov defeated him. The defeat in round five was counted for the medal rounds putting the Soviet Union wrestler ahead. Jadhav's next competitor - Japan's Shohachi Ishii also defeated him. Jadhav, thus bagged the bronze medal and became the first

Indian to win an Olympic medal in an individual sport for independent India.

Jadhav could not try for the 1956 Olympics due to an injury and instead joined as a sub-inspector in the state police in 1955. He resigned in 1983 as an Assistant Commissioner of Police in Maharashtra. He died in an accident at Satara, Maharashtra in 1984.

Jadhav was awarded the Arjuna Award posthumously in 2001. Pune-based writer Sanjay Dudhane came out with a biography on him, titled Olympicveer Khashaba Jadhav, the same year. In 2010, the wrestling stadium at the Indira Gandhi Sports Complex in the national capital was renamed as the K.D. Jadhav Stadium.

K.D. Singh 'Babu', the captain of the 1952 gold medal - winning hockey side, was born on 2nd February 1922 at Barabanki, United Provinces of British India. He received his early education at the Government High School, Barabanki and Kanyakubj Inter College, Lucknow. In hockey, he was initially guided by his elder brother Kr Shukdeo Singh 'Mohan' who was a brilliant hockey player.

Babu's hockey talent was spotted and encouraged by Mushfiq -ur - Zaman, a hockey enthusiast and hotel owner in Aminabad, Lucknow. He first noticed the 14 -year old's talent in 1936 at Shahjahanpur, a district west of Lucknow, in an inter-college match. At the young age of 15, he played for the LYA Club, Lucknow at the Trades Cup in Delhi. In the same Trades Cup, the young team of Lucknow, met with a reputed Delhi team, for which Olympian full-back Mohammed Hussain also played. Hussain was amazed by the hockey skills of the youngster. After the match, Hussain said that K.D.

Singh'Babu' will one day become one of the greatest players of field hockey. K.D. Singh'Babu' not only played for India with great success but also represented Uttar Pradesh in all the National hockey tournaments continuously from 1939 to 1959. He was a talented all round sportsman too.

K.D. Singh 'Babu' was first selected to the All India hockey team in 1946-47 for the tour to Afghanistan. After that there was no looking back and he rose quickly to be one of the deadliest forwards the hockey world has known. In 1947, while playing alongside Dhyan Chand during the East Africa tour, he outscored the wizard by netting 70 goals while the wizard got 62. Even before he was selected as vice-captain of 1948 Olympic team he was being compared to Dhyan Chand. As the team's vice-captain in the 1948 Olympics, he played his part in helping the Indian team win a gold medal at London. Such was his performance in the 1948 Olympics that one of the leading British newspapers wrote: "Babu's performance was as near to perfection as was possible. Scintillating dribbling and adroit through-passes characterized his play and he was the chief instigator in completely tying the dogged England defence. On many occasions he dribbled past the whole defence with ease throughout the tournament. He was the brain behind the attacks. It is tempting to write that Babu is as elusive as Dhyan Chand."

His performance in the 1952 Olympics in which he was the captain was described as 'poetic', where he was the mastermind and playmaker of the team. Former New Zealand captain C V Walter wrote: 'I run out of adjectives in trying to describe his superlative dribbling and the timing and geometrical accuracy of his passing. Babu's dribbling is poetry in motion.' 'Babu' was a born ball player. His sense for tackling a moving ball was amazing. He was nimble on his feet and his reflexes were extremely quick. He was energetic, alert and flexible. Apart from hockey, he also played cricket and tennis well.

As a coach, his reading of the game was fantastic and he could point out the strengths and weaknesses of opponents very accurately. He was much ahead of his time as a coach. He was also an excellent communicator who loved explaining hockey tactics to youngsters and all those who approached him. He served as the coach for the Indian hockey team at the 1972 Munich Olympics.

K.D. Singh 'Babu' received the Helms Trophy in 1953 for being the best hockey player in the world (1952) and the best Sportsman of Asia (1953). This was the first time an Indian was awarded the Helms Trophy. In 1958, he was conferred the Padma Shri by the Government of India. He died unnaturally on 27th March 1978 in Lucknow.

Indian Team: Standing (L to R) Swarup Singh, Keshav Datt, Harbail Singh (Coach), Raghbir Lal Sharma, M L Mitra (Manager), Udham Singh Kullar, Dharam Singh, R S Gentle, Grahanandan (Nandy) Singh, C S Dubey, R Francis.

Kneeling (L to R) Leslie Claudius, Balbir Singh, Meldric St. Clair Daluz, Jaswant Singh Rajput, K.D. Singh 'Babu' (Captain), C Deshamuthu, G Perumal, M Rajagopal, C S Gurung.

Some officials and guests are also seen in the picture.

In the hockey event, twelve teams participated. Eight teams - Austria, Switzerland, Belgium, Finland, Germany, Poland, France and Italy played the preliminary round. The four winners of this round joined India, Great Britain, the Netherlands and Pakistan in the quarter-finals. Eight teams played on a knock-out basis.

India's three rivals on the way to the gold medal were Austria, Great Britain and the Netherlands. On 17th July, India began with a 4-0 win over lowly-placed Austria in the quarter-final. The margin of victory was not satisfactory as many sitters were missed. The forwards were inclined to hang on to the ball. They got a dressing down from the officials, including Raja Bhalindra Singh, G.D. Sondhi and Pankaj Gupta. The officials even picked on some of the established players and told them, "Don't think your place is assured in the team. If you don't play well, we will pack you off." Pankaj Gupta told the players firmly, "I want you boys to play your game, first-time clearances, short passing and nippy thrusts. You know it too well, that's your natural style. No showmanship, mind you."

On 20th July, India was an inspired side against Great Britain in the semi-final. They moved fast and swiftly made inroads into Great Britain's defence. Balbir scored a freak goal as the game began. He out-manoeuvered his rival at the bully-off, rolled the ball between the legs of the centre-half and, as two defenders were standing parallel to each other, he advanced instead of passing to either K.D. Singh 'Babu' or Udham Singh, and his miscued shot foxed the custodian. Balbir scored two more goals to get his hat-trick. This was his second hat-trick in Olympics. The first was in the 1948 London Olympics. On resumption, Great Britain played well and succeeded in narrowing the lead to 1-3 which was the final score.

In the final against the Netherlands on 24th July, skipper K.D. Singh 'Babu' was at his dazzling best. He carved openings and passed the ball to his colleagues without any loss of time. This resulted in India beating the Netherlands 6-1. Apart from K.D. Singh 'Babu', the two wingers, Rajagopal (left) and Raghbir Lal (right) helped India score freely. Balbir again got a hat-trick - his third in Olympics. ***He scored a record 5 goals in an Olympic final.***

Results:

Quarter-final - beat Austria 4-0 (Raghbir Lal Sharma 1, Randhir Singh Gentle 1, Kunwar Digvijay Singh 'Babu' 1, Balbir Singh Dosanjh 1).

Semi-final - beat Great Britain 3-1 (Balbir Singh Dosanjh 3).

Final - beat the Netherlands 6-1 (Balbir Singh Dosanjh 5, Kunwar Digvijay Singh'Babu' 1)

Final Positions - India 1, the Netherlands 2, Great Britain 3, Pakistan 4, Germany 5, Poland 6, Austria 7, Switzerland 8, France 9, Belgium 10, Italy 11, Finland 12.

CHAPTER 7
INDIAN HOCKEY'S POST INDEPENDENCE GOLDEN HAT-TRICK - MELBOURNE 1956

The Indian contingent for the 1956 Melbourne Olympics comprised of 59 participants in 8 sports. This was the first time that the Summer Olympics were held outside Europe. The hockey gold was the only medal India won at Melbourne. The Indian hockey team was led by Balbir Singh, a member of the victorious Indian teams that participated in the 1948 and 1952 Olympics. In the final of the 1952 Olympics, Balbir scored a record 5 goals. Balbir Singh was born on 31st December, 1923 in Haripur Khalsa, Punjab and he passed away on 25th May, 2020 in Mohali. **Balbir was given the honour of being India's flag-bearer in the Opening Ceremonies of the 1952 and 1956 Olympics.**

The Indian hockey team for Melbourne was a mixture of quality experience and talented youngsters. Four of the team - Balbir Singh, Randhir Singh Gentle, Leslie Claudius and Ranganathan Francis - were playing their third Olympics. In addition to other experienced players, there were also some talented youngsters in the squad. The team played four warm - up games in Ambala and Bombay, winning all, but some players stayed out citing injuries. The Indian Hockey Federation ordered fitness tests and Gursevak Singh (PEPSU) was ruled unfit with a dodgy knee and was replaced by Amit Singh Bakshi of the Services on the eve of the team's departure.

BALBIR SINGH DOSANJH
A GREAT OF INDIAN HOCKEY

I was going down the stairs of the V. I. P. pavilion of

the Chandigarh Hockey Stadium after doing the television commentary of the India-Spain hockey test in 2005, when I passed an elderly Sikh gentleman who was sporting the Indian blazer which had 1948, 1952 and 1956 Olympic badges on it. I stopped, looked hard and immediately realised that I was face to face with the great Balbir Singh, one of the two Indian hockey players to have not only won three Olympic Hockey gold medals but also led India in one of those triumphs. The other player to have achieved this feat is the legendary Dhyan Chand in 1928, 1932 and 1936 as captain. **A couple of hours later, I was at Padma Shri Balbir Singh's residence. Our hockey legend kept me spell-bound with his amazing memory and honest and thoughtful observations on the game and the people who ran and played it.**

Who had the greatest influence on your development?

My father, Dalip Singh, was a great person. He was a strict disciplinarian who instilled in me values which helped me to achieve whatever I did in life.

Who was the best coach you have had?

Without doubt, it was the late Harbail Singh. To this day, I am indebted to him for nearly all that I achieved in hockey. Harbail was my coach, mentor, guru, philosopher and guide. He was the one who moulded my game on the right lines.

You were closely associated with Ashwini Kumar - one of India's greatest administrators in hockey. Tell us something about him.

Ashwini Kumar is and was a genius - a brilliant police officer, an outstanding musician, a great writer and, most important of all, a great and lovely human being. He always had in mind what was best for others. He went out of his way to help players. If Punjab became a power to reckon with in the field of sports after partition, it was mainly due to Ashwini Kumar. He played a major role in my grooming, making me a coach at the age of 24. He is and was greatly respected by the players too.

What helped you attain your level of brilliance as a player?

I acquired a great deal of my mobility, agility, wrist work and, above all, quickness of eye by practising with a tennis ball against a wall, when very young.

Your performances in the three Olympics you participated in were remarkable. Please enlighten us.

In the 1948 Olympics at London, I played two matches and scored 8 of the 13 goals, including 2 of the 4 in the final. Four years later, in the Helsinki Olympics, I scored 9 of the 13 goals our team scored in three matches - 3 of my goals were in the semi-final. In the final, I scored 5 out of the 6 goals — a record to date. In the 1956 Melbourne Olympics, where I was fortunate to lead the side, we completed a hat-trick of Olympic gold medals. I played only three games. In the first half of the opening match against Afghanistan, I fractured a finger in my right hand after having scored 5 goals. After that game, I played only in the semi-final and final with a fractured hand.

How did you manage to play such important games with a fractured hand?

For the 1956 Olympics, the Indian side depended a lot on me. So, after my injury in the first match, it was decided that I would play only in the semi-final and final. Each member of the team was told to keep my injury and the doctor's report a closely-guarded secret. Opponents considered me the most dangerous centre-forward of post-war years. The idea of playing me with an injury was to keep defenders on me constantly. In the semi-final, against Germany, the tactic paid off and we won 1-0. Even in the final, Pakistan had two of their defenders on me. This eased the pressure on the inside players. Randhir Singh Gentle, our full back, converted a penalty corner, then called short corner, and we won 1-0.

You have also been a coach and manager of the Indian side. Could you tell us about the great 1975 World Cup win?

The tournament that comes to mind first was our gold medal in the 1975 World Cup at Kuala Lumpur. We were a well-knit unit and the players were greatly helped by Dr. Rajinder Kalra, both physically and psychologically.

What went wrong in the 1982 Delhi Asiad?

The Indian team for the 1982 Asiad was not a bad one. The mauling we suffered at the hands of Pakistan in the final was due to psychological reasons. The team just collapsed that day. Come to think of it that in 1982, India got the bronze medal in the Champions Trophy at Amsterdam and the silver medal in the Esanda Cup at Melbourne. In both the tournaments we beat Pakistan. I was with the team both in Amsterdam and Melbourne.

Who was the best goalkeeper you have played with or against?

Without doubt, it was my Indian teammate, Francis. Everything was perfect about Francis. He was very safe, very cool and possessed excellent reflexes and wonderful anticipation. Francis would not aimlessly kick a ball, instead, he would initiate a counter-attack for his side.

Who was the best back you have played against?

There is no greater challenge for a forward than to beat a cool and tough defender. R. S. Gentle, during my best playing days, was the one who towered above the rest with his hard yet clean tackling. I loved playing against him. In fact, the goals that have given me the most satisfaction have been the ones I have scored with Gentle in the opposition.

Finally, you succeeded Dhyan Chand as India's centre-forward. What was so special about him?

The great Dhyan Chand was much senior to me. However, I have seen him in action. He was a great goal scorer. Apart from his scoring skill, he had masterly control, which enabled him to pass accurately and dribble well.

Indian Team: Standing (L to R) Bakshish Singh, Raghbir Lal Sharma, Charles Stephen, A S Bakshi, R S Bhola, Haripal Kaushik, O. P. Malhotra, Amir Kumar, Balkishan Singh Grewal.

Chairs (L to R) Udham Singh Kullar, Leslie Claudius, Group Captain O.P. Mehra (Manager), Balbir Singh (Captain), Harbail Singh (Coach), R S Gentle, R Francis.

Sitting on the ground (L to R) G. Perumal, Hardyal Singh, Gurdev Singh Kullar, S Laxman.

The Games were marred by boycotts as some of the nations from the Middle East stayed away in the wake of the Suez Canal imbroglio while a couple of European nations, including Spain and the Netherlands, dropped out protesting the Russian handling of the Hungarian Revolution. Consequently, only 12 teams took part. The teams were split into three groups of four each. India (Group A), Great Britain (Group B), and Pakistan and Germany (Group C) advanced to the semi-finals. Two teams from Group C were allowed.

For India, the league phase was a relatively easy affair as they hammered Afghanistan 14-0 on 26th November, the United States of America 16-0 on 28th November and Singapore 6-0 on 30th November. Against Singapore, India took 23 minutes to score its first goal. In the first game against Afganistan, India lost skipper Balbir Singh who suffered a fractured finger. Balbir scored five goals in that match. Randhir Singh Gentle, the ace full-back, captained the side in Balbir's absence. After the first game, Balbir played in the semi-final and final though he was not fully fit.

The India-Germany semi-final on 3rd December was a rough match apart from being poor in quality. The Indians had all the play but the Germans adopted rough and robust tactics while defending the goal. The game was marred by many fouls by the Germans and in one tackle, forward Charles Stephen was felled by a charging defender. He broke his ankle. India, however, prevailed upon Germany 1-0. The goal was scored by Udham Singh Kullar who had a wonderful tournament scoring 14 goals. In contrast, the Great Britain-Pakistan semi-final produced clean and good hockey. Had there been no umpiring lapses, Great Britain might have defeated Pakistan instead of losing 2-3.

Despite Stephen being unavailable and Balbir playing with an injury, India played well against Pakistan in the final on 6th December. India had no weak link either in defence or in the half-line or in attack. Francis was excellent under the bar. Both sides looked tense and this was one of the major reasons for the game not reaching dizzy heights. Both teams resorted to defensive tactics. Attacks never got very far except for sporadic dashes down the wings. In the second half, India was awarded a short-corner and Gentle converted it. After Gentle's goal, Pakistan fought hard and earned a penalty bully. It was ordered to be retaken much to the disappointment of the Pakistan team. Amir Kumar was once again entrusted with the penalty bully from the Indian side. Amir Kumar saved it. So Gentle's goal saw India triumph 1-0. India had won the gold medal again thus completing a hat-trick of Olympic gold medals after independence. **India did not concede a goal in the tournament**.

Results:

League - beat Afganistan 14-0 (Balbir Singh Dosanjh 5, Udham Singh Kullar 4, Randhir Singh Gentle 3, Gurdev Singh Kullar 2).

beat USA 16-0 (Udham Singh Kullar 7, Hardyal Singh Garchey 5, Gurdev Singh Kullar 3, Leslie Claudius 1).

beat Singapore 6-0 (Udham Singh Kullar 2, Charles Stephen 2, Randhir Singh Gentle 1, Hardyal Singh Garchey 1).

Semi-final - beat Germany 1-0 (Udham Singh Kullar 1).

Final - beat Pakistan 1-0 (Randhir Singh Gentle 1).

Final Positions - India 1, Pakistan 2, Germany 3, Great Britain 4, Australia 5, New Zealand 6, Belgium 7, Singapore 8, Malaya (Malaysia) 9, Kenya 10, USA 11, Afghanistan 12.

Randhir Singh Gentle
An Outstanding Full-Back

Randhir Singh Gentle, who was born on 22nd September 1922 in Delhi, was an outstanding full - back. Gentle captained the Indian hockey side in the Melbourne Olympics after skipper Balbir Singh (Sr) was badly injured in the first match against Afghanistan. He captained the Indian side in the remaining matches till the semi-final when Balbir returned to the side. Gentle had the distinction of scoring the decisive goal in the final against Pakistan which gave India the Olympic gold medal for the third successive time after the Second World War.

Gentle shot into the limelight in 1942 when he helped Delhi win the national title. He was a thinking full-back who had mastered the art of the one full-back game when the old off-side rule was prevalent. He used it to great effect for Tatas and Bombay later. Gentle would be the sole defender in his own half, with his colleagues all beyond the half-line. He was considered the cleanest hitter of the hockey ball seen on the playing field. His fluent carpet drives on the bumpy grass grounds were a treat to watch, particularly his hits to the inside-right from his traditional position of left full-back.

Gentle, who was an outstanding full-back, represented India in three Olympics - 1948 at London, 1952 at Helsinki and 1956 at Melbourne. As a full-back, he was feared and respected because of his firm and clean tackling. Balbir Singh (Sr), his captain at Melbourne, rated him as the best full-back he had played against.

He was also a very good umpire and an excellent coach. He coached the Indian team that won the Asian Games hockey title in 1966 at Bangkok for the first time.

Gentle was a role-model to his colleagues and aspiring youngsters as he displayed excellent sportsmanship, high levels of dedication, great playing skills and the attitude of never giving up without a fight. Gentle passed away on 25th September 1981 in Bombay.

Udham Singh Kullar - India's Top Scorer At Melbourne

Udham Singh Kullar, India's top scorer in the 1956 Melbourne Olympics with 14 goals, was born on 4th August 1928 at Sansarpur, a small village near Jalandhar Cantonment of Punjab. He studied at Victor High School and DAV College, Jalandhar. Although Udham had a short stature at just 5 feet 6 inches and weighed only 58 kg, it never affected his game.

He was named the captain of his college hockey team in 1947, and was recruited by the very reputed Punjab Police team the same year. For a period of 18 years he played for Punjab Police and led the team a couple of times during his tenure. Udham Singh Kullar also captained the Punjab State hockey team in 1954.

Udham Singh Kullar would have made his Olympic debut in the London Olympics 1948, but due to a finger injury he missed the chance. He played in a hockey series against Afghanistan in 1949, contributing to India's victory in the series. Udham was a part of the Indian hockey squad at the 1952 Helsinki Olympics, 1956 Melbourne Olympics, 1960 Rome Olympics and 1964 Tokyo Olympics. Alongwith Leslie Claudius, Udham is the only other Indian hockey player to win three Olympic golds and one Olympic silver.

Udham Singh Kullar, was a versatile forward, who could play very well at left-inside, right-inside, centre-forward and even centre-half.

After his retirement from active hockey, Udham engaged in training young boys. He also coached the national teams. To felicitate the services and contribution of Udham Singh Kullar towards the game of hockey, the Government of India conferred on him the Arjuna Award in 1965. Udham died on 23rd March 2000 at Sansarpur, Punjab.

CHAPTER 8
1960 ROME OLYMPICS - INDIA LOSE HOCKEY GOLD

India sent a contingent of 45 participants in 6 sports to the 1960 Rome Olympics. India won only one medal at Rome - a silver in hockey. For the first time in Olympic hockey, India got only a silver medal as the Indian team lost 0-1 to Pakistan in the final. Leslie Claudius, who became the first Indian hockey player to participate in four Olympics at Rome, was the captain of the side. **Claudius was India's flag-bearer at the Opening Ceremony.**

LESLIE CLAUDIUS – FIRST INDIAN HOCKEY PLAYER TO PLAY FOUR OLYMPICS

Padma Shri Leslie Walter Claudius, whom I met for the first time at his spacious flat in central Calcutta in the early 1970s, impressed me at once by his simplicity, friendly behaviour and his love for hockey– a game in whose annals his name is indelibly carved.

Claudius, who played at right-half for India was the first Indian hockey player to represent India in four successive Olympic Games (1948-1960). He and Udham Singh are the only two Indian hockey Olympians to win four Olympic medals- three gold and one silver. **Talking with Claudius on hockey, I soon realized, was an education.**

Claudius was born on 25th March 1927 at Bilaspur. His father worked in the Railways. After studying upto Junior Cambridge at the Railway School, Bilaspur, Claudius joined the Railway Auxiliary Force in 1944. The next year, he played football for the B.N. Railway team in the I.F.A. Shield tournament.

His hockey career began at the age of 19 in 1946 in unusual circumstances. The regular centre-half of the B.N.R. team was injured and Claudius got a chance. That year, B.N.R. lost to Port Commissioners in the final of the Beighton Cup tournament 1-2. It was the first time Claudius played in a Beighton Cup final.

In 1947, when the Railway Auxiliary force was disbanded, Claudius joined the Calcutta Port Commissioners. He made his Bengal debut in 1948. The same year, saw Claudius come into national reckoning. He was a stand-by in the Bengal team that year. Moreover, he saw unable to participate in the Beighton Cup tournament, the same year, as he had a fractured finger. His excellent performances in the Aga Khan Tournament at Bombay earned him a place in the Indian hockey team for the 1948 London Olympic Games.

In 1950, Claudius left the Port Commissioners and joined the Calcutta Customs. In December that year, Claudius was selected to represent the Indian team on a tour of East Africa. In1952, he was a member of the Indian team at the Helsinki Olympics. In 1954, Claudius went to Malaya (Malaysia) with the Indian team. Then in 1955, he toured New Zealand and Australia with an Indian team.

Claudius then represented India in the 1956 Melbourne Olympics – his third successive Olympics. In the Asian Games at Tokyo in 1958, Indian suffered its first setback in international hockey when Pakistan won the title on goal average. I asked Claudius the reasons for India's defeat and he remarked, "The team that represented India had only half a dozen hockey players, while the others, who made the team, had no hockey credentials. About the manager he said, "He did not bother to find out whether the goal average rule would be applied. The draw, too, was arranged in such a way that Pakistan always met a team after India had played against it."

In 1959, Claudius captained the Indian hockey team on their tour of Europe. The team also took part in the Munich Hockey Festival. At Munich, Claudius was adjudged the "Best Player" of the tournament. Claudius captained India in the 1960 Rome Olympics. It was his fourth successive Olympics. That year India lost the title for the first time to Pakistan.

About the Rome Olympics, Claudius said, "It was both the happiest and saddest moments of my life. I was captaining India for the first time in the Olympic Games and it was for the first time, India failed to win the Olympic title. I took the defeat as a slur on my hockey career.

Claudius never recovered from that defeat and did not represent India after 1960. He played for Bengal till 1962 and for Calcutta Customs Club till 1965 - the year in which he received the Beighton Cup winners medal for the first time in his hockey career.

When I asked Claudius which was the most thrilling and exciting match of his career, he said, "The match between the Punjab and Bengal in 1956 Nationals at Jalandhar. In 1952, Bengal had defeated the Punjab in the Nationals at Calcutta. It was for this reason, they wanted to avenge the defeat However, it was not to be. We scored an early goal and then managed to hang on to our lead till the final whistle."

Leslie Claudius was a fine team-man. He was a bundle of energy and a determined fighter who kept his forwards on the move and helped his colleagues in deep defence. He served as a selector and manager at the highest level. He was a gentleman and a true lover of the game.

Claudius was awarded the Banga Bibhushan in 2012. On 20th December 2012, Claudius passed away in Kolkata.

Indian Team: Standing (L to R) Erman Bastian, Prithipal Singh, J Antic, Bandu Patil, Jaswant Singh, Shantaram, Balkishan Singh Grewal, Jhaman Lal Sharma, Kulwant Arora, J Mascarenhas

Chairs (L to R) Official, Udham Singh Kullar, Official, Leslie Claudius (Captain), Official, Haripal Kaushik, R S Bhola.

Sitting on the ground (L to R) Joginder Singh, G Sawant, S Laxman, C Deshamuthu, V J Peter, Mohinder Lal.

Charanjit Singh was injured and so not in the picture.

Of the 44 countries affiliated to the FIH, 27 sought participation in the Rome Olympics. But a maximum number of 16 was allowed to take part in the hockey tournament, held from 26th August to 9th September 1960. The teams were divided in four pools. India was in Pool A. In the four eliminating pools, there were 5 drawn encounters out of 24.

Two replays became necessary before Australia, Germany, Great Britain, India, Kenya, New Zealand, Pakistan and Spain qualified for the quarter-finals. In the concluding eight matches, victory was achieved by a solitary goal every time and in two matches, the game was extended to extra-time. Pakistan looked a fine outfit the moment they defeated the fighting-fit combination of Australia 3-0. India, in turn, defeated Denmark 10-0 in the first match on 27th August and triumphed over the Netherlands 4-1 on 30th August. The Dutch were no pushovers and began in a whirlwind style, snatching the first goal. India, however, stayed undismayed over this reversal and continued playing their polished game as though nothing abnormal had taken place. After equalizing in the first half, they took the field on resumption more determined and more resolute than in the first session. Prithipal and Bhola were on a roll as they netted three goals through penalty corners. Prithipal amply demonstrated what a fine striker of the ball he was. India beat New Zealand 3-0 on 2nd September in its final group match.

In the quarter-final on 5th September, India defeated Australia 1-0 in extra-time and in the semi-final, India got the better of Great Britain 1-0 on 7th September. For India, Bhola scored in the quarter-final while Udham Singh scored in the semi-final.

After 19 games in 10 days, the ground showed signs of wear and tear. In the final, the ground was heavily watered. But both India and Pakistan showed that they could adapt to any pitch - fast, slow, wettish and indifferent. Pakistan launched a full-throttle attack on India. Then came Pakistan's classic goal in the 11th minute. Inside-right Hamid made the move and pushed the ball to the right-winger, Noor Alam who in a flash and a brief run hit the ball to inside-left Ahmed Naseer Bunda (Bunda was his nickname). Naseer stopped the ball dead. His dribble beat Prithipal and with Jhaman Lal Sharma not backing up, the wily Pakistani inside side-stepped the charging Laxman, the goalkeeper, and flicked the ball home. India came back strongly but could not produce the equalizer. There were chances for both teams but no more goals. Pakistan won the gold and India had to be satisfied with the silver.

Results:

League - beat Denmark 10-0 (Prithipal Singh 3, Raghubir Singh Bhola 3, V.J. Peter 2, Jaswant Singh 2).

beat the Netherlands 4-1 (Jaswant Singh 1, Raghubir Singh Bhola 1, Prithipal Singh 2).

beat New Zealand 3-0 (Raghubir Singh Bhola 1, V.J. Peter 1, Jaswant Singh 1).

Quarter-final - beat Australia 1-0 (Raghubir Singh Bhola 1).

Semi-final - beat Great Britain 1-0 (Udham Singh Kullar 1).

Final - lost to Pakistan 0-1.

Final Positions - Pakistan 1, India 2, Spain 3, Great Britain 4, New Zealand 5, Australia 6, Germany/Kenya 7 (joint), the Netherlands 9, France 10, Belgium 11, Poland 12, Italy 13, Japan 14, Switzerland 15, Denmark 16.

CHAPTER 9

INDIA REGAIN HOCKEY GOLD IN 1964 TOKYO OLYMPICS

In 1964, Tokyo in Japan, became the first Asian country to host the Summer Olympics. India's contingent comprised of 53 participants in 8 sports. **Athlete Gurbachan Singh Randhawa was India's flag-bearer for the Opening Ceremony.** The seasoned centre-half Charanjit Singh captained the Indian hockey team which regained the gold - the only medal India won at Tokyo. A write-up on Charanjit follows along with what he shared with me about the Tokyo Olympic hockey final follows:

CHARANJIT SINGH
A FINE CENTRE-HALF AND MATURE LEADER

Charanjit Singh had the honour of captaining the Indian hockey side that regained the gold medal in the 1964 Tokyo Olympics. This mature centre half-back was born on 22nd October 1928 at Mairi village in Una district of Himachal Pradesh. He did his schooling from Khalsa Schools in Gurdaspur and Lyallpur. After that he went on to obtain a B.Sc. (Agri) degree from the Government Agriculture College, Ludhiana. This kind of combination of a scholar and a sportsman is a rare thing. At a very early age, he developed an interest in hockey and was a member of his school team.

In 1949, he played for Punjab University. Charanjit Singh was made the captain of the university team in 1950. He had the good fortune of playing all major tournaments held at that time in the country after joining the Punjab Police in the year 1950. In the year 1958, Charanjit Singh was made the captain of the Punjab State team. The same year, he was included in the national team that toured the country. He then toured Europe in 1959 with the Indian National hockey team.

Charanjit Singh participated at the 1960 Olympics held at Rome. Unfortunately, due to a fractured fibula, he was unable to play the final match against Pakistan. Pakistan defeated India in that game. In the year 1961, Charanjit was made the vice-captain of the National team that toured Australia and New Zealand. He led India to victory in the 1962 International Hockey tournament held in Ahmedabad and represented India in the 1962 Asian Games held in Jakarta. In 1963, he captained the Indian side that toured East Africa and Europe and the one that participated in the Lyons Hockey Festival in France.

In 1964, Charanjit Singh led the Indian hockey team which won the Olympic title in Tokyo. Talking about the win over Pakistan in the 1964 Tokyo Olympics, Charanjit said, "The defeat against Pakistan in the final of the 1960 Olympics at Rome was very much in our minds. I was in that squad. I told my teammates to keep their cool and give their all. Ofcourse, if the need arose we would show the Pakistan team that we could be tough. The entire team rose to the occasion. Ofcourse, Mohinder Lal converted the penalty stroke which proved to be the match-winner. Prithipal Singh, whose penalty corner resulted in the penalty stroke, had a successful tournament both as a defender and as a penalty corner specialist. Laxman at goal brought off some brilliant saves in the last few minutes, in particular, when Pakistan were desperately trying to equalize. It was an unforgettable day for all of us."

Acknowledging his outstanding contribution to hockey, the Indian Government conferred on him the Arjuna Award in 1963 and the Padma Shri in 1964.

Charanjit Singh died on 27th January 2022 in Una, Himachal Pradesh.

Indian Team: Standing (L to R) Harbinder Singh, Joginder Singh, Rajinder Singh, Balbir Singh, Bandu Patil, Gurbux Singh, R.A.Christy, Jagjit Singh, Ali Sayeed, Dharam Singh, Darshan Singh.

Sitting (L to R) Mohinder Lal, Shankar Laxman, Udham Singh, Charanjit Singh (Captain) I.M.Mahajan (Manager), Dharam Singh (Coach), Haripal Kaushik Prithipal Singh, V.J.Peter.

15 countries took part in the hockey event. They were divided into two groups. East Germany played at Tokyo as they had defeated West Germany in a best of 3 play-off. India was in Group B while reigning champions Pakistan were in Group A.

After defeating Belgium in its opening match 2-0 on 11th October, India was held to a 1-1 draw by East Germany on the following day. The India-East Germany match turned out to be a very rough encounter. East Germany took the lead through a penalty corner and in order to defend their lead, the East Germans resorted to very rough tactics. India also played robust hockey. Later in the game, Prithipal equalized for India by converting a penalty corner. Five players – two Indians and three East Germans – were injured.

On 14th October, India unexpectedly drew its next match with Spain 1-1. The Spaniards took advantage of some slack umpiring and resorted to time-wasting tactics soon after taking the lead through a penalty corner conversion. Play became a little rough and in that situation India got a penalty stroke which Mohinder Lal converted.

After having drawn two of its first three group games, India brought in Peter at inside-right and shifted Haripal Kaushik to inside-left. The change made a huge difference to the forward line with India trouncing Hong Kong 6-0 on 15th October, defeating Malaysia 3-1 on 17th October, beating Canada 3-0 on 18th October and getting the better of the Netherlands 2-1 on 19th October. With 12 points from 7 games, India topped its group and had to face Australia in the semi-final.

In the semi-final against Australia on 21st October, Australia took an early lead through inside-left Patrick Nilan but within eight minutes of conceding the goal, India playing brilliant hockey went 3-1 ahead. Prithipal Singh scored twice and Mohinder Lal once. Though Australia played very well in the second-half, the Indian defence held firm. India finally won 3-1 and one more India – Pakistan final was in the offing.

The final between India and Pakistan on 23rd October was delayed as the bronze medal match between Australia and Spain had gone into extra-time. The final was played on a small hockey stadium called Komazawa 1st ground. It could accommodate 3000 spectators in all on the two sides. Pakistan decided to play rough and tough from the start. Their centre-half Anwar Ahmed Khan closely marked India's dangerous centre-forward Harbinder Singh so that

India's movements would be obstructed and restricted. The half-time score was 0-0.

Some five minutes into the second-half, inside-left Haripal Kaushik was obstructed inside the 'D' and India got a penalty corner. Prithipal's powerful hit glanced off goal-keeper Abdul Hamid's pads and struck the foot of right-back Munir Dar. The umpire whistled for a penalty stroke. The 'stroke' was then comparatively new as it had replaced the penalty bully in 1963. Mohinder Lal, taking advantage of goal-keeper Hamid's short height, sent the ball high into the net. India were up 1-0 in the final. Pakistan tried hard to equalize but Laxman at goal was unbeatable. Finally, the Dutch umpire Augustin Lathouwers blew the final whistle and India had regained the Olympic hockey gold.

Results:

League - beat Belgium 2-0 (Prithipal Singh 1, Haripal Kaushik 1).

drew with East Germany 1-1 (Prithipal Singh 1).

drew with Spain 1-1 (Mohinder Lal 1).

beat Hong Kong 6-0 (Prithipal Singh 2, Darshan Singh 2, Harbinder Singh 2).

beat Malaysia 3-1 (Prithipal Singh 2, Harbinder Singh 1).

beat Canada 3-0 (Harbinder Singh 2, Prithipal Singh 1).

beat the Netherlands 2-1 (Prithipal Singh 1, Victor John Peter 1).

Semi-final - beat Australia 3-1(Prithipal Singh 2, Mohinder Lal 1).

Final - beat Pakistan 1-0 (Mohinder Lal 1).

Final Positions - India 1, Pakistan 2, Australia 3, Spain 4, East Germany 5, Kenya 6, the Netherlands 7, Japan 8, Great Britain 9, Malaysia 10, Belgium 11, Rhodesia 12, Canada 13, New Zealand 14, Hong Kong 15.

Mohinder Lal – Scorer Of The Winning Goal In The 1964 Olympics

The Real Club de Polo de Barcelona (Spain) played an exhibition hockey match in Delhi against the IFFCO XI. What struck one most about the Spanish team was that their coach was Mohinder Lal, a former Indian Olympian. Mohinder Lal, who was born on 1st June 1936 at Saharanpur, was a fine half-back in his hey day. He is best remembered for converting the penalty stroke against Pakistan in the finals of the 1964 Tokyo Olympics which won India the Olympic gold after a gap of eight years. He died on 1st July 2004 in Spain. **I met Mohinder Lal at the Shivaji Stadium in the 1980s and spoke with him about his career both as a player and a coach and Indian hockey too.**

Before I ask you anything else, I would like you to tell our readers about that winning goal you scored at Tokyo?

I cannot forget that moment. The penalty stroke was awarded as a penalty corner taken by Prithipal Singh glanced off goalkeeper Abdul Hamid's pads and struck the foot of Pakistan right-back Munir Dar. Much to the relief of the entire side and myself, I converted it. In that tournament I converted all the three strokes I took so I was not nervous at all. This goal of mine gave us the gold which had eluded us in the 1960 Rome Olympics.

When did you qualify as a coach?

In 1963, I did a nine months' coaching diploma from the National Institute of Sports at Patiala.

When did you take to coaching?

While captaining the Northern Railway side, I would, on occasions, give tips as a coach. But I actually started full time coaching when I went to Spain in 1968.

What made you choose Spain?

Actually, I went to Spain in 1968 for treatment of my heart problem which was due to over-exertion. It was while I was there, I got this offer to coach. I have been in Barcelona since then.

Could you tell our readers about the club where you coach?

The club is basically for Polo but it also encourages hockey. It is one of the richest clubs in Europe. It has three hockey grounds – one natural grass, one artificial surface and one all weather.

Finally, what other coaching assignments did you take up in Spain?

I have coached the Spanish Junior National side two or three times in the late seventies. In 1983, I was the coach of the Spanish senior women's side which finished second in the Inter-Continental Championship in Malaysia.

Shankar Laxman
India's Star Hockey Goalkeeper

Shankar Laxman was the goalkeeper of the Indian hockey team in the 1956, 1960 and 1964 Olympics. He won two Olympic gold medals and one silver. He also represented India in the Asian Games in 1958, 1962 and 1966. He was captain in the Indian side that won the 1966 Asian Games hockey title. Laxman retired from the game after he was not selected for the 1968 Olympics. He retired from the Army in 1979 as a captain in the Maratha Light Infantry.

Born at Mhow near Indore on 1st July 1933, Shankar Laxman made his debut in the hockey nationals at Bombay in 1955. He played for the country in the Warsaw Youth Festival that year. He went on to represent the country in both the Asian Games and the Olympics with distinction.

Laxman always kept outstandingly well for India. But his performance in the closing stages of the final against Pakistan in the 1964 Tokyo Olympics will always be fondly remembered. India had taken the lead through a penalty stroke conversion by Mohinder Lal. India, desperately keen to regain the Olympic hockey title which it lost in 1960, did everything to ensure that Pakistan did not equalize. Pakistan bombarded the Indian goal from all angles in order to get the equalizer but Laxman showed courage, agility and uncanny anticipation to prevent Pakistan from equalizing. In the last 10 minutes in particular, Laxman was at his brilliant best thwarting all Pakistan attacks with confidence and grace.

In recognition of his services to the game, Laxman was conferred the Arjuna Award in 1964 and the Padma Shri in 1967. In 2016, he was posthumously given the Major Dhyan Chand Lifetime Achievement Award.

Unfortunately, Laxman who had used his legs to protect India's goal in the Olympics and Asian Games died in Mhow on 29th April 2006 after suffering from gangrene in one leg.

CHAPTER 10
1968 MEXICO - INDIA FAIL TO MAKE HOCKEY FINAL FOR THE FIRST TIME

For the first time in the history of Indian hockey, the Indian hockey side for the 1968 Mexico Olympics had joint captains- Prithipal Singh and Gurbux Singh. India also failed to make it to the Olympic hockey final for the first time. The Indian contingent had 25 participants for 5 games. **Prithipal Singh was India's flag-bearer at the Opening Ceremony.** The hockey team was provided with some high altitude training in the Nilgiris considering the high altitude conditions the team was expected to face in Mexico city. The players benefitted physically but that was offset by many other factors which were unconducive to the team performing well. I will first write about **Prithipal Singh, the joint captain**, and then share an interview of mine with **Gurbux Singh, the other joint captain**.

PRITHIPAL SINGH – A GREAT FULL-BACK AND PENALTY CORNER EXPERT

Prithipal Singh was a deep defender of exceptional skill and ability. He was a quick tackler who distributed passes adroitly. He was a penalty corner expert. Defenders and goal-keepers were afraid of his powerful hits. He was called the 'King of short corners'. In three Olympics, Prithipal Singh scored over 20 goals.

Born at Nankana Sahib, the birth place of the first Sikh Guru, on 28th January 1932, Prithipal Singh announced his arrival at a relatively advanced age of 25 when he played for Punjab in the nationals in 1957. His progress was quick. He impressed everyone with his play. He was chosen to represent the IHF team that toured our country in 1958. In 1959, he was chosen to play for the country on the tour of East Africa. He also participated in the Munich Festival. From there on he did not look back. Prithipal Singh was an automatic choice for the 1960 Rome Olympic Games. He was a member of the Indian team for the 1962 Jakarta Asian Games. Holder of a Master's degree in Agriculture, Prithipal Singh represented India in another two Olympic Games in 1964 (Tokyo) and 1968 (Mexico). In the Tokyo Olympics, he struck brilliant form scoring ten goals – nearly half the goals scored by India. Some of his penalty corners resulted in penalty strokes. For the 1968 Olympics, he was joint captain with Gurbux Singh. He was the first player to receive the Arjuna award when it was instituted in 1961. He was also conferred the Padma Shri in 1967.

Prithipal Singh died under most unfortunate circumstances. He was gunned down by unidentified assailants on 20th May 1983 in the campus of the Punjab Agriculture University (Ludhiana). His death was a great loss to the hockey community in particular and the country in general.

GURBUX SINGH
A PLAYER TOTALLY INVOLVED IN HOCKEY

The other joint captain Gurbux Singh, who was born in Peshawar on 11th February 1936, had the distinction of playing hockey for India, captaining the Indian side and being a coach, selector and manager of Indian teams. He is a person who has given his all to Indian hockey. I wish to add here that Gurbux is perhaps the only Indian hockey Olympian to have played with spectacles. Infact, he even umpired in the 1982 Asian Games. In the 1968 Mexico Olympics he and Harbinder Singh were selected for the World XI. I had done commentary with him during the 1996 Champions Trophy at Chennai and so it was easy asking him to talk about his early career and his stints with the Indian hockey team as a player, captain, coach, manager and umpire.

Who inspired you to take to the game?

My main inspiration was my father Major Kartar Singh. He was my mentor. He was a very good hockey player himself and played for and recruited many promising hockey players to form first of all a strong Indian Hospital Corps (IHC) team in Rawalpindi and later on the Army Medical Corps (AMC) side at Lucknow in the 1950s.

You had the opportunity of seeing the legend Dhyan Chand from close. What impact did he have on you?

In 1959, I was able to observe Dhyan Chand at the national camp which I attended. I witnessed the genius of Dhyan Chand there. His mastery of the bully and the half volley was such that the naked eye could not notice it. Everything was perfect about his game. Infact, he was the greatest and most complete hockey player. He was my inspiration and I was fortunate that he was our coach during the 1963 Lyons tournament.

You made a name for yourself as a hockey player after you came to Kolkata. Please tell readers about the main clubs you played for in Kolkata and their durations.

Yes. I moved to Kolkata in 1956 basically to learn the motor spare parts business with my brother-in-law. I played for East Bengal in the 1957 hockey season. Later in 1957, I joined the Calcutta Customs. I played for Calcutta Customs from 1958 till 1965. While playing for Calcutta Customs, I had the fortune of playing with the great Indian half-back Leslie Claudius. I again played for East Bengal club in 1966 and 1967. From 1968 till 1980 I played for Mohun Bagan. In the 13 years I was associated with the club, we won nine league titles and an equal number of Beighton Cups. Overall, I played in 16 Beighton Cup finals- winning 12 times and finishing runners – up 4 times.

You mentioned about Leslie Claudius. Please tell readers about him.

Leslie Claudius was not only a fine half-back but he was also a true gentleman. His game was simple. He had the knack of being at the right place at the right time. He was the first Indian hockey player to represent India in four Olympics and he had the distinction of captaining India in the 1960 Rome Olympics.

Which are the states you represented in the National Hockey Championships?

I first represented Madhya Bharat in 1955. The great Roop Singh was our coach. From 1957 till 1972 I represented Bengal – captaining it on many occasions. I could not play for my state after that as the IHF made me a national selector in 1973 and insisted on my not playing for my state any more. However, I continued to play local league hockey till 1996 i.e. the age of 61. Here I would like to mention that I first made it to the Indian side during the 1961 New Zealand tour.

You were basically a full-back. How did you end up playing left-half in the 1964 Tokyo Olympics?

Before the 1964 Tokyo Olympics, the Indian hockey side played a three - Test series vs. New Zealand and also toured Malaysia. In the first Test vs. New Zealand, Rajinder

Singh of Railways played at left-half. He failed miserably and India lost 1-3. It was then that the Indian think-tank thought of playing me at left-half. I was nervous as I would have to play at an unfamiliar position and that too in my first Olympics. But, since the team management insisted, I agreed. I performed quite well and India won the next two Tests 5-2 and 8-1. This is how I ended up playing left-half in the 1964 Olympics. We won the gold at Tokyo.

Please tell readers about what happened before and at the 1968 Mexico Olympics where you were the joint captain of the Indian hockey team.

After the 1964 Tokyo Olympics, I wish to state that I captained the Indian hockey side in all main tournaments and matches except for two. The two occasions were first of all, during the 1966 Asian Games when I was expecting to be made captain. To my disappointment, the selectors named goal-keeper Shankar Laxman – a very senior player as captain. They also named three vice-captains – Haripal Kaushik, Prithipal Singh and myself. The second occasion was when I had a broken collar bone in 1967 and so missed the tour to Madrid.

Then came the announcement of the team for the 1968 Mexico Olympics. The team was announced without mentioning the captain and vice-captain. I feel the IHF messed up matters by not taking a firm decision as to who should captain the team. Had they decided on one captain the team would have performed much better. By adopting the compromise formula of naming joint captains – Prithipal Singh and myself, indiscipline crept in and we managed to get only a bronze medal. The only consolation was that centre forward Harbinder Singh and myself were selected for the World XI on the basis of our performances in the Olympics.

Please tell readers about your involvement in hockey after your top playing days i.e. after 1972.

I have been Manager of the Indian side to the Champions Trophy in 1973 and to the Azlan Shah Cup tournament in 1983. In 1974 and 1975 I coached the French national team while in 1976 I was coach of the Indian side that participated in the Montreal Olympics. As an umpire, I officiated in the 1982 Asian Games. Finally, I had five stints as a national selector starting in 1973.

Finally, how has your contribution to the game been recognized?

In 1966, I won the Arjuna Award while in 2013, I was conferred the Banga Bibhushan Award by the West Bengal Government for my outstanding contribution in the field of sports.

Indian Team: Top Row (L to R) Inam-ur-Rehman, P. Krishnamurthy, Gurbaksh Singh, Harmik Singh, R.A.Christy, Munir Sait.

Middle Row (L to R) Dharam Singh, Ajitpal Singh, Tarsem Singh, Inder Singh, Balbir Singh (Railways), Balbir Singh (Punjab), Balbir Singh (Services), Jagjit Singh.

Sitting (L to R) Harbinder Singh, Balkishan Singh (Coach), Prithipal Singh (Joint Captain), Ashwini Kumar (President, I.H.F), Maj. Gen. D.S.Kalha (Manager), Gurbux Singh (Joint Captain), V.J.Peter.

In the hockey event, 16 countries participated. The teams were divided in two pools A and B each having eight teams. India was in Pool A.

In India's first match on 13th October, India suffered a shock 1-2 defeat at the hands of New Zealand. It was the first time in the Olympics India had lost a pool match. India then went on to win all the remaining pool matches. Victories against West Germany (2-1) on 14th October, Mexico (8-0) on 15th October, Spain (1-0) on 17th October and Belgium (2-1) on 18th October put India back on track. India were awarded a 5-0 win though they did not score even one goal when on 20th October, Japan walked out and did not return protesting a penalty stroke awarded against them in the 55th minute of the match. In its concluding encounter on 21st October, India defeated East Germany 1-0 to face Australia in the semi-finals.

In the semi-final on 24th October, India met Australia. Australia started off well subjecting India to a lot of pressure. But against the run of play, India took the lead. Inder Singh scooped the ball towards the goal but Jim Mason raised his stick to slow down the ball. A penalty stroke was awarded and Balbir Singh (Services) converted it. India led 1-0 at half- time. The Australians went into the attack in the second-half forcing two penalty corners. From the second, Brian Glencross scored with a tremendous hit giving goalkeeper Munir Sait no chance. The match went on to extra-time. It was Glencross again who got the winning goal for Australia from a penalty corner.

India then overcame West Germany 2-1 in the bronze medal play-off to finish third. It was the first time that India did not figure in an Olympic hockey final.

Results:

League - lost to New Zealand 1-2 (Prithipal Singh 1).

beat West Germany 2-1 (Harbinder Singh 1, Balbir Singh (Services) 1).

beat Mexico 8-0 (Harbinder Singh 3, Balbir Singh (Services) 1, Prithipal Singh 2, Ajitpal Singh 1, Inder Singh 1).

beat Spain 1-0 (Prithipal Singh 1).

beat Belgium 2-1 (Prithipal Singh 1, Harbinder Singh 1).

beat Japan 5-0 (Walkover given after 55 minutes after Japan walked out in protest so 5 goals were awarded).

beat East Germany 1-0 (Prithipal Singh 1).

Semi-final - lost to Australia 1-2 (Balbir Singh (Services) 1)

Bronze medal playoff - beat West Germany 2-1 (Prithipal Singh 1, Balbir Singh (Railways)1).

Final Positions - Pakistan 1, Australia 2, India 3, West Germany 4, the Netherlands 5, Spain 6, New Zealand 7, Kenya 8, Belgium 9, France 10, East Germany 11, Great Britain 12, Japan 13, Argentina 14, Malaysia 15: Mexico 16.

HARBINDER SINGH
A GREAT HOCKEY CENTRE–FORWARD

Harbinder Singh, an Arjuna Award winner and former three-time Hockey Olympian, was one of the finest centre-forwards our country has ever produced. **In the 1968 Mexico Olympics he was selected to represent the World XI alongwith Gurbux Singh.** Despite his outstanding achievements, Harbinder is most unassuming and modest. A few years back, **I met Harbinder Singh, who was born at Quetta in Pakistan on 8th July 1943 and spoke with him about his career in particular and Indian hockey in general.**

When and how did you take to hockey?

My father, Sardar Balbir Singh, was in the Indian Army. He was an excellent hockey player, who toured Sri Lanka with the legendary Dhyan Chand. So, from childhood we saw a lot of hockey. I picked up the game by watching the army players in action. In school, I played hockey and football with great fervour. Former East Bengal soccer star striker, Gurkripal Singh, played football with me in Jalandhar.

Did the stay in Jalandhar, during your school and college years, help you to become a better hockey player?

Punjab had a very rich hockey culture at that time. Every village would have a number of teams. There would be regular competitions at almost all levels. We became much better players because of the opportunities we got of playing with and observing great players at close range.

At that time, the standard of hockey in the university was also very high. When did you make it to the Punjab University team?

I represented Punjab University from 1959 to 1961. In 1959, I also won a gold medal for the Punjab University Athletics team. In 1961, I was a member of the team which won the inter-university title.

Could you briefly describe your progress in hockey immediately after this?

In 1961, I made my debut for Punjab in the National Hockey Championships. We lost in the final that year but won the title the following year. In the same year, while in my first year in college, I was selected as a member of the Indian Senior Hockey side, which toured New Zealand and Australia.

Please tell readers about your achievements at the national level.

In addition to my being a member of the Punjab side, which won the national title in 1962, I was also a member of the Indian Railways team which won the national title 7 times (5 times in succession from 1963 to 1968). Incidentally, I also won a gold medal while representing the Railways in the 4x100 m relay race in the 1967 National Championship.

What about your achievements at the international level?

I was privileged to represent India thrice in the Olympics and in two Asian Games. We won a gold medal in 1964 at the Tokyo Olympics and a bronze medal each in the 1968 Mexico and 1972 Munich Olympics. In the Asian Games, we won a gold medal in 1966 and a silver medal in 1970 where I captained the side. Both the 1966 and 1970 Asian Games were held in Bangkok.

How did your being a good athlete help your performance in hockey?

Being a good athlete helped me in overtaking or outpacing opposition defenders. On rare occasions, whenever required, I could easily rush back to help my defence.

Which was the most memorable game of your career?

I would rate the 1964 Tokyo Olympics final against Pakistan, which we won, as the most memorable game of my career. It was a crucial game, as we had lost the gold medal to Pakistan in the 1960 Rome Olympics. We just had to win that game. The first 8 to 10 minutes of that game were very rough and played in poor spirit. At that stage, the umpires called both the teams and said that, if the rough play and foul language did not stop, then they would be forced to use red cards. Realising the implication of the warning, both sides then played fast, attacking, brilliant and clean hockey for the rest of the game. We finally managed to win the gold medal. Mohinder Lal, who scored the gold-winning penalty stroke that day, was my room-mate during the Olympics. Earlier, after breakfast, Mohinder Lal had told me that he had dreamt that India would be awarded a penalty stroke in the final. He also told me that the Pakistan goalkeeper was short. So, if a penalty stroke was awarded, he would place the ball over the goalkeeper's head. As fate would have it, Mohinder Lal's dream came true! He got the chance to do as he had planned in the morning, and India won the gold medal.

Which was your most memorable tournament?

The 1968 Olympics at Mexico was my most memorable tournament. I was the second top scorer. I was also selected in the World XI at the conclusion of the tournament.

Who was the best goalkeeper you have played against?

Norihiko Matsumoto - the Japanese goalkeeper in the 1968 Mexico Olympics was, without doubt, the best goal-keeper I have played against. We could not score against him. Of course, our own Shankar Laxman was also superb. Talking about Laxman, I cannot forget the three successive saves he brought off in the last two minutes of the 1964 Tokyo Olympics final against Pakistan. Laxman first saved a direct hit, then a rebound and then another rebound which followed immediately after.

Who was the best defender you have played against?

Without doubt, it was our own Prithipal Singh. He was the best player of the 1960 Rome Olympics. He was a good full-back, with a very commanding personality. His penalty corner conversions were superb. Such was his presence, that the forwards in the opposition would shy away from him.

CHAPTER 11

BRONZE AGAIN FOR INDIAN HOCKEY AT MUNICH

The Indian hockey side won India's only medal in the 1972 Olympics in Munich, West Germany. For the second time in a row in the Olympics, India got a bronze medal in hockey. For India, 41 competitors took part in 7 sports. **Indian footballer and Boxing official Brig. Devine Jones was India's flag-bearer at the Opening Ceremony.**

The Indian hockey team to the Munich Olympics sported a new look with only four players from the 1968 edition making the cut. Among those making their Olympic debut for India was Ashok Kumar, son of legendary Dhyan Chand. The competitions in the Munich Olympics were overshadowed by the Palestinian terrorist attack on Israeli athletes, 11 of whom were gunned down. The hockey tournament saw the end of Asian dominance in the Olympics as Germany displaced Pakistan as the new champions. The captain of the Indian side was Harmik Singh.

HARMIK SINGH
AN EXPERIENCED LEFT HALF-BACK

Harmik Singh, who was born on 10th June, 1945 in Gujranwala, Punjab was an experienced player who captained the side. He was a member of the Indian side which won medals in all major tournaments from the 1966 Asian Games till the 1974 Asian Games. In the 1968 and 1972 Olympics in which he represented the country, India won the bronze medals. He was a member of the bronze medal and silver medal winning teams in the 1971 and 1973 World

Cup tournaments respectively. In the Asian Games, he was a member of the India teams which won the gold in 1966 at Bangkok and silver medals in 1970 at Bangkok and in 1974 at Tehran. He also captained the Asian All-Star Team against the European XI in Brussels. He was conferred the Arjuna Award in 1997 and his reaction was "Better late than never". **My interview with Harmik follows:**

Please tell readers about your family and its involvement in hockey.

My father, late Shri Sohan Singh was a reputed hockey player and my mother Satwant Kaur was a house wife. My father's brother late Shri Sahib Singh was an Indian hockey player of high repute. In my family, we are four brothers, who have all actively played hockey. The family has three Olympians - my younger brother Ajit Singh, his son Gagan Ajit Singh and myself. Ours is the second family after Dhyan Chand, Roop Singh and Ashok Kumar to have made a mark for India in international hockey.

How and when did you take to hockey?

The family's passion and involvement motivated me to actively indulge in the game from the age of 10 to 12 years.

Who was your first coach? Please name the other coaches.

I picked up the skills of the game from my father and my uncle and my school teacher Giani Balbir Singh in Ferozepur.

When and how did you make it to the senior Indian side?

As a student of DAV College, Jalandhar, I played for

the Combined Universities in the Nehru Memorial Hockey tournament and came into the limelight. I was picked up for the Senior National Hockey camp for the Bangkok Asian Games in 1966. I made the final side.

Finally, why did we only get the bronze medal in the 1972 Olympics?

The 1972 Olympic hockey team was a young and capable side focussed on winning the tournament. It was a very close fight with Pakistan in the semi-final. We got 14 chances including 9 penalty corners but it was just not our day as we dominated most of the second half. Pakistan's two goals in the first half proved decisive.

Indian Team: Standing (L to R) M. Frederick, Harbinder Singh, Aslam Sher Khan, Harcharan Singh, Mukhbain Singh, Harmik Singh (Captain), Ajitpal Singh, Kulwant Singh, Charles Cornelius, M. P. Ganesh, Vece Paes.

Kneeling (L to R) V. J. Phillips, Varinder Singh, B P Govinda, P Krishnamurthy, Ajit Singh, Ashok Kumar, M. Kindo.

At Munich, 16 teams participated. India was placed in Group B in the hockey event. The team played seven group matches in nine days on most occasions on very uneven surfaces. In one or two games, rain made the surface very difficult to play on. On 27th August, India played its first group match against the Netherlands. The match was keenly fought. The Netherlands took the lead in the very first minute. India managed to equalize through Ashok Kumar in the 29th minute. The final score was 1-1. In the next game on 28th August, India scored a convincing 5-0 win over Great Britain. India led 4-0 at half-time thanks to three penalty corner conversions by Mukhbain Singh. The other goal was scored by Michael Kindo. In the second half, India scored only one more goal through skipper Harmik Singh. India then played Australia on 30th August. Mukhbain Singh was again in good form with his penalty corners scoring a hat-trick. Australia's only goal came after Mukhbain Singh's second penalty corner conversion. India thus scored an impressive 3-1 win over a tough Australian side.

India drew 2-2 with Poland in the next game on 31st August. The match was played on an uneven field which became very soggy due to rain. Good hockey was difficult. India led 1-0 at half-time through Harmik Singh. Early in the second half, Poland scored two quick goals to take a 2-1 lead. In the 50th minute Govinda equalized for India.

A strong Kenya side consisting of many players of Indian origin gave India a tough fight in the next match on 2nd September. Kenya led 1-0 at half-time. After Mukhbain Singh's equalizer early in the second - half, Kenya once again took the lead in the 45th minute. India fought back to win the game 3-2 thanks to goals by Harmik Singh and Mukhbain Singh.

The following day, India scored an easy 8-0 win over Mexico. India's final group match on 4th September was against New Zealand. India managed to win a tough encounter 3-2. New Zealand took the lead and because of Kulwant's equalizer the score at half-time was 1-1. The second half saw three goals. Ganesh first put India in the lead. Then New Zealand equalized once again. But within a few minutes Michael Kindo scored what turned out to be the winning goal.

India lost to Pakistan 0-2 in the semi-final on 8th September. India missed 14 chances including 9 penalty corners. Pakistan took a 2-0 first-half lead through Fazalur Rehman and Shahnaz. Since Mukhbain Singh had been very successful with his penalty corner conversion, the Pakistan team used the speedy Isla-ud-din to upset his rhythm when taking penalty corners. The tactic proved a success. In the bronze medal play-off on 10th September, India once again met the Netherlands. As in the first group match, the Netherlands took an early lead this time in the 6th minute. India equalized through Govinda in the 15th minute. The game was evenly contested. In the final minute of the match, Mukhbain Singh converted a penalty corner to give India a 2-1 win and the bronze medal. India, thus earned a hockey bronze for the second successive Olympics. Mukhbain finished with 9 goals in the tournament.

Results:

League - drew with the Netherlands 1-1 (Ashok Kumar 1).

beat Great Britain 5-0 (Mukhbain Singh 3, Michael Kindo 1, Harmik Singh 1).

beat Australia 3-1 (Mukhbain Singh 3).

drew with Poland 2-2 (Harmik Singh 1, Govinda 1).

beat Kenya 3-2 (Mukhbain Singh 2, Harmik Singh 1).

beat Mexico 8-0 (Kulwant Singh 3, Ashok Kumar 2, Harmik Singh 1, Michael Kindo 1, Govinda 1).

beat New Zealand 3-2 (Kulwant Singh 1, Ganesh 1, Michael Kindo 1).

Semi-final - lost to Pakistan 0-2.

Bronze medal play-off - beat the Netherlands 2-1 (Govinda 1, Mukhbain Singh 1).

Final Positions - West Germany 1, Pakistan 2, India 3, the Netherlands 4, Australia 5, Great Britain 6, Spain 7, Malaysia 8, New Zealand 9, Belgium 10, Poland 11, France 12, Kenya 13, Argentina 14, Uganda 15, Mexico 16.

MUKHBAIN SINGH
INDIA'S TOP GOAL SCORER

Mukhbain Singh, the top scorer for India with 9 goals in the 1972 Munich Olympics, was born on 12th December, 1944 in village Shatab Garh, Sialkot, West Punjab, Pakistan. He migrated to Gurdaspur with his parents S. Darbara Singh and Surinder Kaur after partition in 1947. He passed his matriculation from Guru Nanak Khalsa High School, Batala, Gurdaspur, Punjab in India. While playing for his school, he was selected in the district team and from there was selected for the Punjab side. In 1965, he joined the Railway Protection Force as a sub-inspector against the sports quota. **I spoke with Mukhbain, who retired from the Railway**

Protection Force in Ferozepur as a Divisional Security Commissioner in 2002, about his early hockey career, his achievements and the Munich Olympics.

How did you take to hockey?

Hockey was in our family. My father played hockey for the Indian Army and also played with Dada Dhyan Chand.

Who coached you?

My first coach was S. Dharam Singh (Sr.) who represented India in the 1952 Olympic Games. Later I trained under Dada Dhyan Chand in the Railways.

Which are the state sides you played for?

When I started my career, I played for Punjab. After joining the Railways in 1965, I played for the Northern Railways and the Indian Railways till 1982.

Why was your international career limited to only one Asian Games and one Olympics?

I was at the peak of my fitness and career when I missed the 1966 Asian Games being a standby. I played the pre-Olympics in 1967 in London and missed the 1968 Olympics because I offended a very senior hockey official by joining the Railways instead of Punjab Police/BSF. Later I represented India in the 1970 Asian Games and the 1972 Olympic Games.

Why and how did we lose to Pakistan in the semi-finals of the Munich Olympics?

We lost to Pakistan because we failed to convert our chances. We earned 9 penalty corners and were not able to convert any. I took 6 shots and 3 were taken by Michael Kindo. Later, Pakistan's senior player - Tanveer

Dar confessed to me that their only plan was to just stop our penalty corner conversions. Isla-ud-din was given the job to prevent our team from converting penalty corners. We also missed 5 other chances.

Please elaborate on your hat-trick vs Australia?

I noticed that the Australian goalkeeper came forward during penalty corners. So, I hit hard ensuring that the ball struck the boards at both corners of the goal. In those days, to score goals one had to ensure that the direct hits sounded the cage boards as balls hitting the goal-netting were disallowed. Only rebound hits were given as goals if they struck the goal-netting.

How were you honoured for your services to the game?

I won the best Sports Person of the Year award for the Railways in 1973 and the Dhyan Chand Award for Life Time Achievement from the President of India in 2008.

CHAPTER 12
1980 MOSCOW OLYMPICS - INDIA WINS HOCKEY GOLD AFTER 16 YEARS

The gold medal which the Indian hockey team won at the 1980 Moscow Olympics was the only medal the Indian contingent won in the Games. India had 76 participants who took part in 4 sports. **Shooter Randhir Singh was India's flag-bearer at the Opening Ceremony.**

After the hockey debacle at the 1976 Montreal Olympics, India fielded a relatively young but talented side for the Moscow Games, where barring skipper Vasudevan Baskaran and goalkeeper Bir Bahadur Chhetri, the rest made their debut. The Games was marred by a U.S. - led boycott over the Russian presence in Afghanistan which led to many top teams not participating.

VASUDEVAN BASKARAN
AN EXPERIENCED PLAYER

V. Baskaran, the captain of the side, was born in Tiruvannamalai in Tamil Nadu on 17th August, 1950. He was basically a centre-half who could play in other positions keeping the needs of the team in mind. He also represented India in the 1976 Olympics, 1973 and 1978 World Cup tournaments and the 1974 and

1978 Asian Games. He also coached the Indian side in major competitions. He was the first Indian to become an FIH Grade I Coach in 1985-86. Baskaran, a graduate in Economics from Loyola College, Chennai retired from the Southern Railway as Senior Manager, HR/Sports. He was conferred by the Government of India the Arjuna Award in 1979 and the Padma Shri in 1981. **I spoke with Baskaran on his early years, his hockey playing and coaching career and finally on Indian hockey.**

Please tell readers about your family and their involvement in hockey.

My father P. Vasudevan was a national champion in pole vault and a decent hockey player. All my four brothers played hockey at the national level. V. Prabakaran, the eldest, played for India and represented Tamil Nadu in 16 nationals - captaining 6 times. My elder brother V. Rajasekaran played for India and the Indian Railways in 11 nationals. My younger brother V. Jayasekaran played for India and Tamil Nadu and finally my youngest brother V. Vasikaran also played for Tamil Nadu.

When and how did you take to playing hockey?

Hockey was very popular in those days and so everyone took to school, hockey sticks along with their school bags. My elder brothers motivated me to play hockey and so I started playing the game when I was 9 years old.

Who was your first coach? Please name your other coaches too.

My first coach was Mr. Kesavan – a Sports Council Coach. Later, Mr. Kishan Lal, the Indian captain in the 1948 Olympics, was my coach. Otherwise, Mr. Balkishan Singh, a former Olympian and coach, was my favourite coach.

When did you first represent your state at the senior level? Which other states did you play for?

I played for Madras from 1970 till 1973. From 1974 till 1987 I played for the Indian Railways.

Please tell readers about the 1980 Olympics where India won the gold with you as the captain.

Our team, despite been very inexperienced, played confident hockey without showing any pressure. It was a very fine team effort as we won some very tough and close games. Md. Shahid was outstanding while Surinder Singh Sodhi scored a record 15 goals.

Finally, for how long did you coach the Indian side?

My first main assignment as coach was during the 1987 Junior World Cup when we won the silver medal. I have also coached the national side in the World Cup (1998, 2006), 2 Champions Trophy tournaments, the 2000 Sydney Olympics and the 2006 Asian Games.

Indian Team: Standing (L to R): Surinder Singh Sodhi, Rajinder Singh, Davinder Singh, Vasudevan Baskaran

(Captain), Dayanand (Manager), Mr. Balkishan Singh (Coach), Charanjit Kumar, Md. Shahid, Gurmail Singh, A.S.Rana.

Kneeling (L to R) Mervyn Fernandis, Ravinder Pal Singh, Zafar Iqbal. Bir Bahadur Chhetri, Allan Schofield, M.K.Kaushik, M.M.Somaya, S.Dung Dung.

The men's hockey competition was reduced to six teams due to the boycott and so the competition was played on a league basis with the top two teams making it to the final.

India made an encouraging start as they defeated Tanzania 18-0 in the opening match on 20th July. Surinder Singh Sodhi scored 5 goals while Davinder Singh and Baskaran got 4 each. India's happiness was however short-lived as the title aspirants were lucky to draw with Poland 2-2 on the following day. There were some agonising moments as India were in danger of losing. India's equalizer came in the dying minutes of the match. In command for most of the match, India had to wait for 32 minutes to score their first goal through Davinder Singh who converted a penalty corner. On resumption, India earned a penalty stroke, but Baskaran's push was stopped by the goal-keeper. Encouraged by this, Poland restored parity through a penalty corner. In the 30th minute, Poland forged ahead through a penalty stroke. In the dying minutes of the game, Mervyn Fernandis scored following a penalty corner melee, to the relief of all Indians.

India again dropped a point when they were held by Spain 2-2 on 23rd July. India were the first to score in the 15th minute when Surinder Singh Sodhi shot in. Undismayed by this reversal, Spain rallied brilliantly. They netted two goals in quick succession to go into the lead. India then earned three penalty corners and eventually succeeded in equalizing through Sodhi. In the concluding four minutes, India made efforts to get another goal but in vain. The following day, India trounced Cuba 13-0. Surinder Singh Sodhi scored 4 goals.

In the concluding league match on 26th July, India defeated the Soviet Union 4-2, to finish second to Spain in the league. India made a rousing start with Davinder Singh converting a penalty corner in the 3rd minute. The exchanges were fast and evenly balanced. The Soviet Union tried their best to restore parity, but they could not. A minute from half-time, India consolidated their position when Surinder Singh Sodhi converted a penalty stroke.

On resumption, the Soviet Union reduced the lead. India came back strongly and scored again in the 6th minute. This goal came following their fifth penalty corner. Davinder's shot was saved by the goalkeeper. M.K. Kaushik, standing unmarked, shot in and the custodian stopped it. When he was clearing it, he was penalised for 'sticks'. This resulted in a penalty stroke and Sodhi made no mistake to put India 3-1 ahead. India kept attacking the Soviet Union goal. Most of the moves were initiated by Md. Shahid. Only six minutes remained when the Soviet Union reduced the lead. India then scored again through M.K. Kaushik to win the match 4-2.

On 29th July the final was played between Indian and Spain at the Dynamo Minor Stadium. India went into the lead in the 24th minute when Surinder Singh Sodhi converted a penalty stroke. Six minutes later Sodhi scored again. This time it was a field goal. M.K. Kaushik scored the third goal on resumption. Spain then fought back. Their veteran back and penalty corner expert Juan Amat made it 2-3. In a counter attack, India made it 4-2 through Md. Shahid but Juan Amat made it 3-4 completing a hat-trick in the process. There was excitement in the stands as only five minutes remained. Spain forced two penalty corners but goalkeeper

Chhetri was upto it. India were home with the gold after encountering some nasty moments. The Olympic gold was India's after 16 years.

In 1964 at Tokyo, G.D. Sondhi, then the member of the IOC, presented the Olympic gold medal to the Indian team, led by Charanjit Singh. At Moscow, this great honour went to Ashwini Kumar, the IOC executive committee member. Baskaran was the proud Indian captain.

Results :

League - beat Tanzania 18-0 (Surinder Singh Sodhi 5, Davinder Singh 4, V. Baskaran 4, Zafar Iqbal 2, Md. Shahid 1, Mervyn Fernandis 1, M.K. Kaushik 1).

drew with Poland 2-2 (Davinder Singh 1, Mervyn Fernandis 1).

drew with Spain 2-2 (Surinder Singh Sodhi 2).

beat Cuba 13-0 (Surinder Singh Sodhi 4, Md. Shahid 2, Davinder Singh 2, Rajinder Singh 2, Amarjit Rana 2, V. Baskaran 1).

beat the Soviet Union 4-2 (Davinder Singh 1, Surinder Singh Sodhi 2, M.K. Kaushik 1).

Final - beat Spain 4-3 (Surinder Singh Sodhi 2, M.K. Kaushik 1, Md. Shahid 1).

Final Positions - India 1, Spain 2, Soviet Union 3, Poland 4, Cuba 5, Tanzania 6.

SURINDER SINGH SODHI
INDIA'S TOP SCORER AT MOSCOW

Surinder Singh Sodhi, who was born on 22nd June, 1957 in Ferozepur, was the top scorer in the 1980 Summer Olympics at Moscow with 15 goals. He bettered Udham Singh's 14 goals in the 1956 Melbourne Summer Olympics. Surinder has also represented the country in the World Cup tournaments in 1978 and 1982 at Buenos Aires and Mumbai respectively, Champions Trophy in 1980 at Karachi and 1982 at Amstelveen where he was the captain – the team won a bronze medal and in the 1978 Asian Games at Bangkok where India won a silver medal. After being initially named captain of the Indian side for the 1982 New Delhi Asian Games he was suddenly dropped from the side just before thc Games. Surinder became a conferred IPS Officer in 1995 and retired in 2016 as Inspector General of Police GRP Punjab. Being a fine officer, he was awarded the Kathin Police Sewa Medal in 1993 and the Police Medal for Meritorious Service in 1994. The Government of India conferred on him the Arjuna Award in 1997. **I spoke with Surinder about how he took to the game and the memorable moments of his career.**

When did you start playing hockey seriously?

I started playing hockey seriously in school. I studied at the Doaba Khalsa School, Jalandhar. Believe it or not, I even made the Indian side while in school. This was in 1975, when I toured New Zealand as a member of the Indian hockey side. Since then, I have been playing quite regularly for the country.

Your playing for India, while still at school, is obviously quite an achievement. Surinder, who was your coach?

My coach was the well-known Gurcharan Singh Bodhi, the Assistant Coach of the Indian side which won the 1975 World Cup tournament.

Please describe the great match against Pakistan in the Champions Trophy at Amstelveen in 1982?

It was a great match which was played at a tremendously fast pace. We were down 0-3 after 16 minutes and we recovered to win 5-4. Veterans rated that match as the best of the century. Also, remember it was our first win in a tournament against Pakistan after many years.

Please tell readers about the 15 goals you scored in the 1980 Moscow Summer Olympics which played a big role in India winning the Olympic Gold medal after 16 years.

Our team played co-ordinated hockey with the forwards moving with perfect understanding. Shahid, in particular, was outstanding in creating goal-scoring opportunities. Of the 15 goals I scored, the more important ones were the two goals against Spain in the league phase which we drew 2-2, the two goals against the Soviet Union in our 4-2 win in another league match and finally the first two goals against Spain in the final which we won 4-3. I also wish to add that in the match against Tanzania I scored 5 goals including a hat-trick. My hat-trick came in 8 minutes.

Finally, which game of yours would you rate as your best?

I have played really well in a number of big games but the match which stands out is the final of the 1980 Summer

Olympics where India defeated Spain 4-3. I put India 2-0 ahead in the final and finished the tournament with 15 goals.

Md. Shahid
The Architect Of India's Moscow Win

Mohammad Shahid, who was born on 14th April 1960 in Varanasi, was one of the finest inside forwards the world has seen. He was given 'the Best Forward' award in the 1980 Champions Trophy. He was selected for the World XI after the Champions Trophy in Amstelveen in 1982. His skill and ability at the 1986 Seoul Asian Games earned him a place in the Asian All-Star team that year. According to Zafar Iqbal, when

India defeated Spain 4-3 in the final of the 1980 Moscow Olympics, Shahid not only scored an important goal but with his brilliance he set-up fellow team-mates to score. The Olympic gold we won in the 1980 Olympics would have been near impossible to achieve but for Shahid. Opposition teams put so much focus on him that other Indian forwards benefitted. Shahid was conferred the Arjuna Award in 1980 and the Padma Shri in 1986. He died on 20th July 2016 in Gurgaon due to a serious liver ailment. **My interview with Shahid which was taken by me many years back follows:**

Shahid, how did you take to playing hockey?

For me it was the easiest thing possible as our family is deeply interested in the game. My father was a useful player while my brother. Asmatullah. has played for UP in the National Hockey Championship.

Were you coached by anybody?

I was extremely lucky to have been trained by Jhaman Lal Sharma, a former Indian hockey international. Mr Sharma helped me a lot in improving my game.

When did you first play for your state?

I made my debut for U.P. in the National Hockey Championships in 1978. at the age of 18. I played for U.P. in the following year too, before joining the Railways. Since 1980, I have been playing for the Railways.

When did you first play international hockey?

I got my first taste of international hockey in 1979. when I was selected to represent India in the Junior World Cup tournament at Versailles. The next year, I made my international debut in the senior level too, when I was selected to represent the Indian senior side in the Quadrangular at Kuala Lumpur.

Which game will you rate as your most memorable one?

Obviously, the match against Pakistan in the Champions Trophy at Amstelveen in 1982. After 16 minutes play, we were down 0-3 but thanks to our team's never-say-die spirit and Rajinder's superb hat trick we managed to win 5-4.

Your combination with Zafar lqbal makes India's left flank one of the best in the world today. How has this come about?

Zafar bhai is a good elder brother to me. Moreover. having played together since 1980. we have developed a great understanding. Fortunately, both of us have talents which, when used together, can shatter any defence in the world.

Finally, what are the qualities that go to make an outstanding inside-forward?

To be a good inside forward, one has to possess the qualities of stick-work, body dodge and the art of combination with the wings and halves.

CHAPTER 13

LEANDER PAES GETS INDIA ITS FIRST INDIVIDUAL OLYMPIC MEDAL IN 44 YEARS AT ATLANTA

Leander Paes's bronze medal in the men's tennis singles event on 3rd August was India's only medal in the 1996 Olympics in Atlanta. USA. It had been 44 years since an Indian last won an individual medal in the Olympics. K.D. Jadhav earned a bronze medal in the Wrestling freestyle bantamweight category at the 1952 Helsinki Olympics. Paes's medal was also India's first since their men's hockey team won the gold in the 1980 Moscow Olympics. At Atlanta, India drew a blank in hockey getting no medal. India had 49 participants in 13 sports. **Hockey star Pargat Singh was India's flag- bearer at the Opening Ceremony.**

LEANDER PAES
AN OUTSTANDING AND AGELESS TENNIS PRO

Leander Paes was born on 17th June 1973, in Kolkata and studied at La Martiniere Boys' School, Kolkata. He has won 18 Grand Slams titles (8 men's doubles and 10 mixed doubles). His mixed doubles Wimbledon title in 2010 made him the second man after Rod Laver to win Wimbledon titles in three decades. He won a bronze medal for India in singles in the 1996 Atlanta Olympic Games. He competed in consecutive Olympic appearances from

1992 to 2016, making him the first Indian and only tennis player to compete at seven Olympic Games. He is a former Indian Davis Cup team captain and holds the record for the most Davis Cup doubles wins - 43 - surpassing Nicola Pietrangeli who had 42 victories. The Government of India conferred on him the Arjuna Award in 1990, the Rajiv Gandhi Khel Ratna Award in 1996, the Padma Shri in 2001 and the Padma Bhushan in 2014. **I contacted Leander through his father Dr. Vece Paes to know about Leander's early career, achievements and tennis in general.**

What was the influence of your parents on you in bringing about a sports culture?

My parents always had an early influence on my sporting culture as my mother Jennifer captained the Indian national basketball team in the Asian Championship in 1982 and my father Vece played field hockey for India in the first World Cup in Barcelona in 1971 and the Munich Olympics in 1972. In fact, through my parents' encouragement, I used to play sports nearly every day.

What made you take to tennis and when did you join organised tennis training for the first time?

I was playing tennis from the age of five (1978) as part of my general sporting pursuit training under Anwar Ali at Calcutta South Club. At the age of 9, I developed convulsions and hence had to avoid football and contact sports. Very reluctantly, I took up tennis. I began to enjoy playing the game and at the age of 12, I joined professional tennis in the Britannia Amritraj Trust (BAT) in Chennai run by Mrs Maggie Amritraj and Vijay Amritraj and sponsored by Britannia's.

Please tell readers about the time you spent at the Britannia Amritraj Trust (BAT).

Coach Akhtar Ali introduced me to Vijay and Anand Amritraj and recommended that I be given a trial for the BAT academy. Anand played with me and was impressed with my competitiveness and athletic ability. In April, they invited me to join the BAT academy. The BAT academy was easily the best and most professional tennis academy at that time in India. Mrs Maggie Amritraj ran a tight ship and was very strict with the eight of us. Vijay and Anand used to come to Chennai regularly to play with us and monitor our progress. Besides, we had three outstanding dedicated coaches in Dave O'Mera, Ted Murray and Indian coach T. Chandrasekaran. We practised every day including Sundays. We joined the Madras Christian College, where the Principal, Mr Felix, gave us terrific encouragement - arranging for tutors etc.

Please tell readers about the individual Olympic medal you won for India in 1996.

I entered the 1996 Atlanta Games as a wild-card. In the first match of my Olympic campaign, I lost my opening set 6-7 to Richey Reneberg of USA but from there I fought all odds and won eight straight sets against Reneberg 7-6, 1-0 - retired, Nicolas Pereira of Venezuela 6-2, 6-3, Thomas Enqvist of Sweden 7-5, 7-6 and Renzo Furlan of Italy 6-1, 7-5 to set up my semi-final clash with Andre Agassi. I lost to Agassi 6-7, 3-6 and so met Fernando Meligeni for the bronze medal. Against Meligeni on 3rd August, I was one set down but I fought on and rallied from behind to defeat the Brazillian 3-6, 6-2, 6-4 to take home the bronze medal. In the process, I became the first Indian to win an individual Olympic medal since wrestler K.D.Jadhav won a bronze at the 1952 Helsinki Olympics. It was both a historic and great moment for me. I was fortunate to have my family and friends present there to witness my achievement.

Please tell readers about three of your most memorable singles wins in big tournaments.

The first one is without doubt my win over Fernando Meligeni of Brazil which helped me earn an Olympic bronze medal in the 1996 Atlanta Olympics. The second memorable win of my career was in August 1998 when I defeated Pete Sampras 6-3, 6-4 in the third round of the Pilot Pen International tournament at New Haven, Connecticut, USA in my only meeting against him in my career. Though it took place earlier in 1990, my third most memorable win was when I won the Junior Wimbledon title to be ranked Junior No. 1 in the world.

Please recall for readers two of your most memorable Davis Cup performances.

There are two performances that straightaway come to mind. The first one was in 1993 when India played France in the Davis Cup quarter-final at Frejus. I won both my singles against top French players Arnaud Boetsch (6-4, 7-5, 6-4) and Henri Leconte (6-1, 6-2, 3-6, 6-3) on a slow clay court. Ramesh Krishnan won the fifth match and by winning the rubber 3-2, India had achieved one of the great victories in Davis Cup.

The second was in 1995 against Croatia at New Delhi. I played in all the three matches India won. In the first singles, I defeated Sasa Hirszon 6-3, 6-3, 6-4 while in the doubles Mahesh Bhupathi and I achieved our first Davis Cup win defeating Goran Ivanisevic and Sasa Hirszon 4-6, 7-5, 6-3, 7-6. Then, despite being ranked 123 in the world, I defeated World No. 7 Goran Ivanisevic 6-7, 4-6, 7-6, 6-4, 6-1 to help India win the tie.

Who is the best doubles partner you have played with in (a) men's doubles and (b) mixed doubles?

This is a difficult question because over the years I have had over 100 partners and many of them were outstanding. If I am forced to choose, in the men's doubles it would be Radek Stepanek of Czech Republic. I won two Grand Slam titles with him i.e Australian Open 2012 and US Open 2013. In the 2012 Australian Open, Stepanek and I defeated the third, second and top seeds on the way to winning the title.

In the mixed doubles, it is a toss-up between Martina Navratilova and Martina Hingis. Martina Navratilova and I won the 2003 Australian Open and 2003 Wimbledon. Martina, at that stage, had the most wins in singles and doubles and with that win at Wimbledon, she was winning the most mixed doubles. Martina Hingis and I were a top class mixed doubles team. We won three of the four Grand Slams in 2015 - Australian Open, Wimbledon and US Open and another one in 2016 at the French Open.

It was a great experience playing with both of them. They also liked playing with me.

What has kept you going so long without ever letting your standards or enthusiasm drop?

Tennis is a great game and allows you to play longer than contact sports. Besides, I love competing in the clean environment of professional tennis. I know that at some time I will have to retire but in the meantime, I am enjoying myself. The game has evolved so much that I have reinvented myself may be 11, 12, 13, 14 times. I have added power to my services in only the last two years to keep up with the young guns by stepping up my training regime. The game and I are very respectful of each other. Besides, it kind of shows when people love coming out to watch me play and cheer.

Why has India not produced a really top-level singles player since Ramanathan Krishnan?

I feel the reasons for this are first of all, the game has become very physical and our singles players cannot compete at a high level of physicality. Secondly, in the period of 18-24 years when one is developing one's skills, we Indians lack the long term focus and the money to pay for it all. Thirdly, the Indian player in most sports is easily satisfied and does not target the very top as there are soft alternatives such as joining the American university circuit.

CHAPTER 14
KARNAM MALLESWARI - INDIA'S ONLY MEDAL WINNER AT SYDNEY

Karnam Malleswari's bronze medal in the women's 69 kg event in Weightlifting on 19th September was the only medal won by India in the 2000 Olympics at Sydney in Australia. **It was for the first time that an Indian woman won an Olympic medal.** In hockey, India once again got no medal. 65 participants represented India in 8 sports. **Leander Paes was India's flag - bearer for the Opening Ceremony.**

KARNAM MALLESWARI – FIRST INDIAN WOMAN TO WIN AN OLYMPIC MEDAL

Karnam Malleswari who was born on 1st June 1975 in a small village called Voosavanipeta in Andhra Pradesh, has the distinction of being the first Indian woman to win

an Olympic medal. She achieved that distinction when she won a bronze medal in the weightlifting event (69 kg. category) at the 2000 Sydney Olympics. Apart from being the world champion in 1994 and 1995, she won silver medals in the 1994 Hiroshima and 1998 Bangkok Asian Games. The Government of India conferred on her the Arjuna Award in 1994, the Rajiv Gandhi Khel Ratna Award in 1995 and the Padma Shri in 1999. **I met Karnam at**

her office in New Delhi and spoke with her about how she took to the sport, her Olympic medal and Indian weightlifting.

By whom and when was your talent for weightlifting first noticed?

My elder sister who was six years older than me was an athlete who trained at the local stadium. Some coaches felt she could be a good weightlifter and so asked her to take to the sport. I used to go with her to the stadium but the coach felt that I was not cut out for weightlifting. I was hurt and so I learnt on my own. My sister was invited to a camp in Bengaluru in 1989. I accompanied her. Many weightlifters were there and I used to closely observe them in order to pick up the finer points. A Russian coach was there at the camp. It was mainly because of him I became a weightlifter. He had observed my keenness to learn and so he gave me a trial. He was satisfied and told the chief coach to include me in the national camp. He even trained me for about eight to nine months. This was how I got into weightlifting.

What was your first major success that put you in the limelight?

I came into the limelight in the junior nationals at Udaipur in 1990 where I won three gold medals and set nine national records. After that there was no looking back.

How did you prepare yourself for the 2000 Sydney Olympics where you won a historic medal?

For the 2000 Sydney Olympics, I trained with one objective in mind – to win the gold medal. I wanted to be an inspiration to all Indian women who took to sports. In 1998, I suffered a back injury. My husband Rajesh Tyagi, a national weightlifter, ensured that I had the best treatment. He helped me to recover as quickly as possible and also helped me with my training keeping the Olympics in mind. All the weightlifters for the Sydney Olympics underwent serious training at Patiala. I was also helped by the Russian coach Leonid Taranenko.

Please tell readers about the bronze medal you won in the 2000 Sydney Olympics.

I trained for the Sydney Olympics with the aim of winning the gold. The Sydney Games was my first international meet after moving up to 69 kg from 54 kg. I could have won the gold that day i.e 19th September. I lifted 110 kg in the snatch. In the clean and jerk, I started with 125 kg and then lifted 130 kg Unfortunately, there was a miscalculation on the part of my coaches which resulted in my lifting 137.5 kg in my last attempt to be in gold medal contention. I was not successful. In actual fact, I could have won the gold if I had lifted 132 kg i.e. an extra 2 kg instead. I still regret not winning the gold but my only satisfaction is that I had become the first Indian woman to win an Olympic medal.

What must be done by India to win medals in Olympic weightlifting?

Weightlifting is not a sport that people particularly the well-to-do ones crave to take up. It is taken up by the poor or lower middle class people in our country. Again, only when someone achieves something do people who matter show interest. No one bothers about the grassroots level infrastructure, coaching and training facilities. People do not realize that lifting weights and practising 10 to 12 hours a day is both physically and mentally very tough. The Government is trying to do its best. I feel people with money and interest in sports must ensure that budding weightlifters have the best infrastructure and coaching from an early age. There should be quality academies all over the country so that we can produce Olympic medal winners regularly.

Karnam, how are you doing your bit in this regard?

Wishing to help our country produce Olympic medallists in this sport, my husband Rakesh Tyagi and I conceptualized and launched India's first Weightlifting and Powerlifting Academy in Yamunanagar, Haryana in March 2017. We are also being helped by the Ministry of Sports and Youth Affairs, Government of India and the Sports Authority of India. The trainees are from rural and underprivileged backgrounds. They are provided with a gymnasium, a perfect training area, most modern equipment, best possible coaching and nutritional support. My husband and I regularly visit the academy to ensure that the highest standards are maintained.

CHAPTER 15

RAJYAVARDHAN SINGH RATHORE'S MEDAL - INDIA'S SILVER LINING AT ATHENS

For the third successive Olympics, India won only one medal - Rajyavardhan Singh Rathore winning the silver in the men's double - trap event in Shooting on 17th August in the 2004 Summer Olympics at Athens, Greece. The Indian hockey side once again failed to get a medal. India sent 73 participants in 14 sports. **Athlete Anju Bobby George was India's flag - bearer at the Opening Ceremony.**

RAJYAVARDHAN SINGH RATHORE - FIRST INDIAN SHOOTER TO WIN AN OLYMPIC MEDAL

Col Rajyavardhan Singh Rathore became the first Indian shooter to win an Olympic medal (a silver) on 17th August in the 2004 Athens Olympics. **I met Col Rathore in Delhi and asked him about his early life, how he took to shooting, his Olympic medal and what he felt about the sport in India.**

Please tell readers about your early background and the sporting interests of your younger days.

I was born on 29th January 1970 at Jaisalmer. My father was a Colonel in the army while my mother has been a teacher. The two sports I liked a lot when young were shooting and cricket.

What made you take up shooting ahead of cricket?

You will be surprised to know that I was about to make it to the Madhya Pradesh Ranji Trophy team when I was only in class 10. My mother told me not to go for the trials as she was keen that I complete my basic education. I then joined the NDA (National Defence Academy) where slowly but surely my interest and progress in shooting grew.

When did you take to shooting seriously?

My studies at the Indian Military Academy where I won the 'Sword of Honour' and then my stint in Kargil and other duties made me take up shooting seriously as a sport as late as 1998. But since 1998, it was only hard scientific training and rigorous practice.

How did you qualify for the 2004 Athens Olympics?

I had achieved a lot of success in different competitions all over the world. However, my bronze medal at the World Championship in Cyprus helped me to qualify for the 2004 Olympics.

Please tell readers about how you won the Olympic silver medal.

At Athens, I finished fifth in the qualification to make the double - trap final. The windy conditions had upset my rhythm. In the final, with UAE's Ahmed Al Maktoum almost certain to win the gold, the silver medal came down to a fight between China's Wang Zheng and myself. In the end, I was left needing to shoot both the flying clay targets in my last attempt to take the silver medal. I managed to stay calm and so succeeded in destroying both the targets. I had won the Olympic silver medal much to my joy and that of millions of Indians. I finished with 179 (135+44) as against Zheng's 178 (137+41).

At the presentation there was a sight which all Indians still remember - your draping the country's flag around you. What were your thoughts then?

I wanted something close to a symbol which represented my country and I felt that our national flag was the best possible thing. So I wrapped the National flag all around me. I cannot say how inspired and thrilled I felt that time.

Which other performance after the Olympics do you remember with great fondness.

Though I have had notable successes before and after my 2004 Olympic feat, I remember fondly the first Asian Shot Gun Shooting Championship at Kuala Lumpur in 2011. In that competition. I equalled Russian Vitaly Fokeer's mark set at the World Cup held in Concepcion, Chile in March 2011 and won the gold medal in the double-trap event. In the team event of which I was a member we won the bronze. The individual performance of mine is an event I will always remember as my ability and temperament were really tested.

What honours have been conferred on you because of your achievements in the sport 'Shooting'?

The Indian Army with whom I am serving have given also possible recognition. They have also provided me with all possible assistance in my training, practice and facilities. The Government of India conferred on me the Arjuna Award in 2003 and the Rajiv Khel Ratna in 2004.

What special qualities are required to win an Olympic medal-a silver in your case?

First of all, an individual must have a personal hunger to achieve. He or she needs to be perfect technique-wise and most important of all unruffled in tight and tense situations.

Here I wish to mention that our culture and religious books provide a lot of wisdom which if appropriately applied brings success. The goal must be clearly defined and we must work unrelentingly towards it, with total focus. Finally, if we have the blessings of elders and God is with us, success is assured.

Finally, you passed through a tough period in 2009 and 2010 when you were about to quit the sport due to a number of reasons. Who stood by you then?

For helping me to continue in the game first and foremost I must thank my family. My wife was and is a great pillar of strength. In fact, she has been a friend and philosopher. Honestly, it feels good that even if you do not have faith in yourself, there are others who have faith in you.

CHAPTER 16

ABHINAV BINDRA'S GOLD SHINES AMONG INDIA'S THREE MEDALS AT BEIJING

The 2008 Beijing Olympics witnessed the best ever performance by an Indian contingent (consisting of 56 participants in 12 sports) in terms of medals. India finished with three medals - one gold and two bronze - which bettered its two silver in 1900 and the gold and silver won in the 1952 Olympics. **India's flag-bearer at the Opening Ceremony was the shooter Rajyavardhan Singh Rathore.**

India won its first ever individual Olympic gold when Abhinav Bindra won the men's 10m air rifle event on 11th August. Bindra's gold was India's first medal at Beijing. On 20th August, Vijender Singh won a bronze medal in the middleweight 75 kg category event in Boxing after losing in the semi-final. It was India's first ever Olympic medal in Boxing. The next day wrestler Sushil Kumar won a bronze medal in the men's freestyle 66 kg category event to become India's second wrestling Olympic medal winner after K D Jadhav's bronze in the 1952 Olympics. In Hockey, our men's team did not participate for the first time since the 1928 Olympics as it did not qualify.

ABHINAV BINDRA - INDIA'S 1ST INDIVIDUAL OLYMPIC GOLD MEDALLIST

Abhinav Bindra, who was born on 28th September 1982 in Dehradun, became India's first individual Olympic gold medal winner when he won the 10m air rifle event at the 2008 Beijing Olympics. Abhinav is an inspiration to all young Indians who wish to win medals in the Olympics. **I met Abhinav in Delhi and spoke with him on Shooting, his Olympic gold medal and sports in India in general.**

After your disappointment in the Athens Olympics, how did you prepare yourself for the Beijing Olympics?

After the disappointment at Athens, I started reappraising and reshaping myself as a shooter. The only thing of concern to me was winning the Olympic gold. I would only be thinking about Shooting. I wanted to go into the 2008 Olympics having made it so tough for myself (working hard on practice, physical fitness and mental toughness) that nothing I faced would hurt. So thoroughly had I been trained that when I arrived in Beijing I had no fear.

Please tell readers about how you won the Olympic gold.

At Athens, my body language had been defensive but at Beijing, I was most positive, aggressive and confident. I was fourth among those who qualified for the final. Henri Hakkinen of Finland at 598 was first, followed by the defending Olympic champion Zhu Qinan of China at 597, Alin George Moldoveanu of Romania and myself at 596. I had a few problems with my sighting shots but my first shot of the final was 10.7. I was third after the first shot, second after the third shot, leading after the seventh shot and tied with Hakkinen at the top after the ninth shot. My final shot fetched 10.8 and I finished with 700.5. With Hakkinen shooting 9.7 a few seconds later, I won a historic gold medal - the first ever individual one for India in the Olympics. Zhu Qinan's final shot fetched 10.5 and he finished with 699.7 to get the silver while Hakkinen with 699.4 got the bronze.

What were your feelings after you won the gold medal?

I was relieved, contented and satisfied after my achievement. I was also proud as I had become the first Indian to achieve that feat. I was grateful to God that my continuous hard work and preparation had paid off. Honestly, I had prepared hard to perform well – winning the gold medal was an unbelievably great moment for me.

What does one generally need to do to become an Olympic champion?

The most important things a person must have or do to become an Olympic champion are first of all to possess the will to succeed, to work very hard, persevere, persist and develop the ability to absorb failure. Of course, one has to have the mental fortitude but it will always be a combination of one's technical skills which must be strong, and one's physical fitness and durability for one to succeed. The mental part also cannot be neglected. At the end, one has to get everything right together to be successful. I followed the holistic approach to my training concentrating on all three aspects – technical, physical and mental.

What do you feel must be done by India so that it becomes a sporting nation?

First of all, our Government needs to decide whether we want to become a sporting nation and whether Olympic sports are a priority. If, they are, then we need to invest in them. We need to have patience and we need to invest long term. Top class coaches who are dedicated and have an eye for talent have to be recruited. Then games have to be started and developed from the grassroots level. The process of talent spotting and grooming should follow. But, the problem in India has been that we wake up to Olympic sports once in four years. When the Olympics come, the media and the public show interest. If we do not get results, there is disappointment which is first followed by negativity and then total quiet. So, we first of all need to decide whether we wish to become a sporting nation and whether Olympic sports do mean a lot to us. Then the other things will automatically follow.

How, according to you, should sports be a part of school education?

Schools must ensure that the physical education teachers selected are ones who are not only passionate about the sports they have specialized in but also possess the ability and keenness to spot and groom genuine talent. Primary and even middle level teachers must be interested in sports. Of course, sports must be an essential part of the curriculum with children playing atleast three to four games at the primary level mainly for fun. Proper incentives must be given to excellent sports persons and the school authorities must ensure that the lost academics of these sports persons are made up. Again, once children start loving sports, the values which sports teaches must be inculcated in them.

Finally, what are the benefits one gets from Shooting as a sport?

The great thing about the sport is that we concentrate on and aim at getting better and better. The sport helps us to focus better and goes a long way in improving our mind and body coordination.

VIJENDER SINGH – FIRST INDIAN BOXER TO WIN AN OLYMPIC MEDAL

Vijender Singh Beniwal better known as Vijender Singh became a professional boxer in 2015. He holds the distinction of being the first Indian boxer to win an Olympic medal. He achieved this distinction in the 2008 Beijing Olympics when he defeated Carlos Go'ngora of Equador 9-4 in the quarter-final of the middleweight division. **I had the good fortune of speaking with this humble, cultured and high quality boxer about his early days in the sport, his international successes and Indian boxing.**

When and how did you take to boxing?

I was born on 29th October 1985 in a village called Kaluwas. In the village there was nothing to do except fighting or wrestling. One day I went to Bhiwani with the intention of taking up hockey. Hockey sticks were expensive and so I did not pursue the sport. I then thought of taking up gymnastics. After seeing people do it, I felt it was not the sport for me. When I was leaving I saw 10 to 15 boys shadow-boxing. I got interested and started copying them. I imitated them well and the coach Jagdish Singh was impressed. He told me to come everyday. He was a very strict coach and he was the person who inspired me to take up boxing seriously. My elder brother Manoj was also a boxer but it was God who drew me to the sport.

How did your boxing talent get noticed?

I started practising regularly at the Bhiwani Boxing Club under the watchful and caring eyes of coach Jagdish

Singh, a former national level boxer. I won a silver medal in my first sub-junior nationals in 1997 and went on to bag my first gold medal at the 2000 Nationals. In 2003, I became the all India youth boxing champion. However, it was during the 2003 Afro-Asian Games, my talent got noticed at the All India level. Despite being a junior boxer, I won a silver medal in my event.

Please tell readers about your main successes in the big international competitions till your medal-winning performance in the 2008 Beijing Olympics.

In 2004, I competed in the Athens Olympics in the welterweight division. I was young and inexperienced then and so I lost early. In the 2006 Melbourne Commonwealth Games, I got a bronze medal. Before the 2006 Doha Asian Games, I decided to move up in weight and took part in the middleweight (75 kg) division at the Doha Games. I won a bronze medal.

How did you prepare yourself for the 2008 Beijing Olympics?

I followed a rigorous training schedule and a well worked out practice match schedule as part of my preparations for the 2008 Beijing Olympics. I also spent some time early in 2008 in Germany training with the German boxers. I even took part in a tournament in Germany which had boxers from all over Europe. At the President's Cup boxing tournament which is said to be a dress-rehearsal for the Olympics, I defeated Kazakhstan's Bakhtiyar Artayev in a quarter-final bout. My performance made me confident of my physical shape. After the exposure in Germany, my training continued in Patiala where I along with other Olympic bound boxers attended a camp. Video recordings of my likely opponents at Beijing were shown to me with analysis of their techniques and manoeuvres.

Please tell readers about how you became India's first boxer to win an Olympic medal at Beijing in 2008.

At the 2008 Beijing Olympics, I was a more mature and experienced boxer. In the round of 32, I defeated Badou Jack of Gambia 13-2. Then in the round of 16, I defeated Angkhan Chomphuphuang of Thailand 13-3 to reach the middleweight boxing quarter-finals. The Thai boxer's elbow technique injured me on the left side and I had a lot of treatment before the quarter-final. In the quarter-final, I defeated Carlos Go'ngora of Equador 9-4 to assure myself of a medal. In the semi-final, I threw everything at my opponent Emilio Correa of Cuba, but he stood tall and I lost 5-8 and shared the bronze. This was the most memorable moment of my life as I became the first Indian boxer to win an Olympic medal.

What were your successes after the Beijing Olympics and before you became a professional in 2015?

In the 2009 World Amateur Championships, I got a bronze medal in the 75 kg middleweight category. The following year, I got a silver medal in the invitational Champion of Champions boxing tournament in China. Again, in the 2010 Delhi Commonwealth Games, I got a bronze medal. In the 2010 Guangzhou Asian Games, I defeated two-time world champion Abbos Atoev of Uzbekistan 7-0 in the final and won the gold medal. After losing in the quarter-final of the 2012 London Olympics, I won a silver medal in the 2014 Glasgow Commonwealth Games.

Who are the people who have helped you become a top-level boxer?

I owe my achievements to a number of people. They are Mr. Jagdish Singh - my first coach, my family, friends and my sparring partners without whom it would have been almost impossible to achieve what I have.

What qualities must a person possess to become a top-level boxer?

To become a top-level boxer one has to work very hard and seriously on technique and fitness. However, the most important thing is to train using one's mind i.e. to think differently. One should not blindly follow orders or instructions.

How can Indian boxers win many more medals in the Olympics?

Our boxers need to be original in their thinking. Again, they need more exposure. Our coaches are as good as the foreign ones. Lastly, the medical facilities which our players get are not upto the mark. This results in our boxers not being physically at their best when required.

You became a professional boxer in 2015. Please tell readers what professional boxing is and your experience as a professional boxer.

My experience as a professional boxer has been good as I have to date (end of July 2019) a 11-0 record. This kind of boxing needs more hard work and patience as the fights are of 10/12 rounds. Lastly, professional boxing is more brutal.

Finally, how did the Government of India recognize your contribution to the game?

The Government of India conferred on the Rajiv Gandhi Khel Ratna Award in 2009 and the Padma Shri in 2010.

SUSHIL KUMAR – SECOND INDIAN WRESTLER TO WIN AN OLYMPIC MEDAL

In the Beijing Olympics, Sushil Kumar won the bronze medal in the freestyle 66 kg category. He became the second Indian wrestler to win an Olympic medal after K D Jadhav in the 1952 Olympics. **I met Sushil at his Delhi office. To his credit, despite his very busy schedule, Sushil spoke in detail about his early life, the people who helped him grow in the sport and how he has been able to do well.**

Sushil, please tell readers about your early life and how you took to wrestling.

I was born on 26th May 1983 in Baprola, Delhi. I was inspired to take up wrestling by my father Mr. Diwan Singh and cousin Sandeep. Sandeep sacrificed his career to help me take up wrestling seriously. This was how I took to wrestling.

Where did you first train to become a wrestler and who were your coaches?

I started training at the Chhatrasal Stadium's akhada in Delhi at the age of 14. I was trained at the akhada by coaches Yashvir ji and Ramphal ji and later by Satpal ji.

Is wrestling a violent sport?

Wrestling has very clearly defined rules. Sometimes, in the spirit of competition, people get hurt. But, it is not a violent sport.

What lessons did you learn after training in the akhada?

Apart from learning the art of wrestling, we learnt discipline, respect for elders and loyalty. We were made to realize that to do well, one had to be keen and determined to succeed. Hard work, perseverance and belief in oneself were a must if one wished to reach the top. To become a top-class wrestler one has to have all these traits.

What is your training schedule like?

We train in two sessions- morning and evening for three hours each. Wrestling requires a significant amount of cardio-vascular endurance. Our workout programme includes different exercises and rope climbing too to build strength and endurance. For developing stamina, we play other games too like Basketball, Volleyball, Badminton and Football. We also have to ensure that we have the right diet and take sufficient rest.

What role has your family played in your achievements as a wrestler?

Right from the time I started taking wrestling seriously, my family has done everything possible to ensure that I succeed as a wrestler. My cousin Sandeep gave up wrestling so that I could take to the sport. My parents would ensure even till the 2008 Olympics that I would have the necessary dietary supplements by sending me the best milk, ghee and vegetables. I am a strict vegetarian. Their sacrifices and blessings have helped me a lot in my progress. One of my coaches Satpal ji, a fine wrestler himself, not only coached me but also served as a friend, philosopher and guide. I am fortunate he is my father-in-law. So I have the support of all my family members.

What were your main successes at the junior level in international wrestling?

My first success came at the 1998 World Cadet Games in Moscow when I won the gold medal in my weight category. Honestly, it gave me the feeling that I could win medals- even golds- at the international stage. This was followed by another gold medal in the 2000 Asian Junior Wrestling Championship in New Delhi. This win convinced me that I could do India proud at the international level-juniors and seniors.

At the senior level what were your medal- winning performances before the bronze you won at the Beijing Olympics in 2008?

In 2003, I won the bronze medal at the Asian Wrestling Championship in New Delhi. The same year, I won a gold at the Commonwealth Wrestling Championship in London. I again won gold medals in the Commonwealth Wrestling Championships in 2005 at Capetown and in 2007 at London.

Please tell readers about the bronze medal you won at the 2008 Beijing Olympics.

My first Olympics was in 2004 at Athens. I was a youngster then and participating in the Olympics that year overawed me. I was placed 14th in the 60 kg weight class. I learnt a lot at Athens and prepared myself well for the 2008 Olympics. The international competitive exposure before the 2008 Olympics helped me a lot. In the 2008 Olympics, I took part in the 66 kg weight category event. My campaign at Beijing seemed over when I lost in the first round to the eventual silver medallist Andriy Stadnik of Ukraine 1-8 but repechage provided me a ray of hope. My best form returned and I defeated American Doug Schwab 7-4, Albert Batyrov of Belarus 8-4 and finally the losing semi-finalist Leonid Spiridonov of Kazakhistan 3-2 to win the bronze medal. It was a great moment for me and millions of Indian fans as my medal was only India's second Olympic medal in Wrestling after K D Jadhav's bronze in the 1952 Helsinki Games.

How have you been honoured for your services to the sport?

The Government of India conferred on me the Arjuna Award in 2005, the Rajiv Gandhi Khel Ratna Award in 2009 and the Padma Shri in 2011.

CHAPTER 17

INDIA DOUBLES BEIJING MEDAL TALLY AT LONDON

For the 2012 London Olympics, India sent 83 participants who competed in 13 sports. The men's field hockey team again participated after not having qualified for the 2008 Beijing Olympics. The team finished 12th (last) in the hockey event. India also marked its Olympic return in Weightlifting. The International Weightlifting Federation had imposed a two-year suspension for Indian weightlifters in Beijing because of a doping scandal. **Sushil Kumar was India's flag-bearer at the Opening Ceremony.**

This was India's most successful Olympics in terms of total medal tally. India finished with 6 medals (2 silver and 4 bronze) doubling the previous record of 3 medals (1 gold and 2 bronze) at the 2008 Beijing Olympics. India's medal winners were shooters Gagan Narang (a bronze) on 30th July and Vijay Kumar (a silver) on 3rd August, badminton star Saina Nehwal (a bronze) on 4th August, boxer Mary Kom (a bronze) on 8th August and wrestlers Yogeshwar Dutt (a bronze) on 11th August and Sushil Kumar (a silver) on 12th August. Sushil Kumar became the first Indian to win medals in successive Olympics having won a bronze at Beijing. Saina Nehwal became the first Indian man or woman to win an Olympic medal in Badminton while Mary Kom became the first Indian woman boxer to win an Olympic medal.

Gagan Narang
India's First Medal Winner At London

Gagan Narang, who was born on 6th May 1983 in Chennai, became India's first medal winner at the 2012 London Olympics when he won a bronze medal in the men's 10 m air rifle event on 30th July. In addition to this prestigious medal, Gagan has also won a number of medals in different international shooting competitions all over the world. The Government of India conferred on him the Arjuna Award in 2005, the Rajiv Gandhi Khel Ratna Award for 2010 and the Padma Shri in 2011. **I spoke with Gagan on his early shooting career, his Olympic medal-winning medal effort and Indian shooting.**

When and how did you take to shooting?

I took to shooting at the age of ten - shooting balloons with a toy pistol on the Marina Beach in Chennai on one of my visits there with my parents.

Who were your coaches?

My first coach was Niranjan Reddy and then Sanjay Chakravarty. Subsequently, I have worked with several national and international coaches. The Indian team has had a few foreign coaches like Laslo Czusak, Stanislav Lapidus with whom I have had the chance of working with.

What were your main achievements at the international level?

At the international level, I have won one Olympic medal, one World Championship medal, six World Cup medals, including one in the World Cup finals. I also have ten Commonwealth Games medals and five Asian Games medals. I have shot 600/600 - a world record in the air rifle event a few times. It is the perfect score.

How did you prepare yourself for the Olympics in which you won a medal?

The preparation happened over a cycle of four years. I followed an Olympic training programme that was charted out by my then coach – Stanislav Lapidus. I also had the funding support from the Government of India and Olympic Gold Quest to see through the entire plan- from drawing board to the Olympic podium.

Please* describe how you won the bronze medal in *the London Olympics.

In the qualifying stage, I came 3rd with a total of 598/600 and made it to the final round of the 10m air rifle event. The weight of expectations following Abhinav Bindra's exit intensified as every Indian pinned hopes on me for a medal. All the hours of hard work I had put in paid off in the final on 30th July. I demonstrated tremendous temperament and resolve to hold my nerve in a tense climax that witnessed the competitors' rankings including that of the top three change with every shot. In the end, I managed to keep China's Wang Tao, who was hot on my heels in the final, at bay and finish with a total score of 701.1 to earn a bronze and become India's first medal winner at the 2012 Games. I finished just behind silver medallist Niccolo Campriani of Italy who scored 701.5. The gold medallist was Romania's

Alin George Moldoveanu with 702.1. I was really happy to win an Olympic medal as that was the only medal I did not have in my cabinet.

When did you take to coaching?

I am not into coaching actively. I only do my work with Gagan Narang Sports Promotion Foundation, that runs sixteen Gun for Glory academies across the country. There are coaches at the Gun For Glory academies. My role is more of mentorship and ensuring the all round development of the kids. I try and help them develop personal mastery.

What qualities must one possess to win a medal in the Olympics?

To win an Olympic medal, one needs to have a high level of aspiration, grit and the ability to put in hours and hours of hard work.

What are your observations on the progress made by Indian shooters in the last two decades or so - the emergence of young champions.

Indian shooting has progressed leaps and bounds. Today, the ranges are bursting in their seams. There are many kids who come in, register and do well initially, then fizzle out. The others that are more tenacious stay on. Many are there dreaming the Olympic dream. So the sport as such is in a very healthy state.

Finally, what is your take on foreign coaches?

The recent performances of the young brigade suggest that our coaches should get a chance. The earlier we start the better. We should depend on foreign experts in areas where we do not have depth. Also, foreign coaches should share their knowledge with national coaches to improve the coaching standard.

Vijay Kumar – London Olympic Shooting Silver Medallist

Vijay Kumar, who was born on 19th August 1985 in Harsaur Village, Himachal Pradesh, won the silver medal in the 25m rapid fire pistol event in the 2012 London Olympics. **I met Vijay Kumar in Delhi and spoke with him about his shooting career and the Olympic medal he won in London.**

Could you tell us about your life till you joined the Army?

My father served in the Indian Army. Though we were not very well off, my father inculcated a deep sense of values in us. After completing my formal education, I joined the Indian Army at the age of 18 in order to fulfill my dream of joining the army and also support my family.

What role has the army played in your development as a shooter?

Whatever I am today is largely due to the Indian Army. Initially, it was after joining the Army that I was able to sharpen my shooting skills. In a few years, I became the best pistol shooter in the Army and started winning competitions both at Army and national levels. The Army has provided all of us with a top class foreign coach Pavel Smirnov. I am particularly happy that he will be around for another four years. The Army ensures that we get the best equipment with ammunition and training facilities including foreign exposure.

Which coach of yours has had the greatest impact on you and your development?

Without doubt, it has been Pavel Smirnov. He plans out everything for me from general training to improvement in technique. Before the London Olympics for example, he had worked out everything so well that I peaked at the right time – the shooting event in the London Olympics. In my best interest, he was very strict about my activities. For instance, four months prior to the London Olympics, when we were rigorously training in Europe picking up vital tips on competition and acclimatizing to the conditions, I was not allowed to make or take more than one call a day. Shooting was not to be discussed in those calls. The isolation was complete when a fortnight before the Olympics the facebook and twitter accounts were deactivated.

What is your normal training schedule?

I usually train for six to seven hours a day. I also do physical training for about two hours daily. Apart from this, when I feel free I also enjoy playing badminton, table tennis and billiards. I also like cycling.

Please tell readers about how you won the silver medal at the London Olympics.

I made it to London after clinching a silver at the ISSF World Cup in Fort Benning, USA in 2011. On 3rd August, I made it to the final of the 25m rapid fire pistol event. I scored 585/600 to finish fourth among the six finalists. The final round comprised of 8 rounds of 5 shots each making it a total of 40 shots. The world champion - Russian Alexei Klimov faded out of contention. After a 3 in round one, Cuba's Leuris Pupo got 3 perfect fives to lead after the first four rounds on 18 with China's Ding Feng and myself tied for the second spot on 16. Pupo, Ding Feng and myself all scored 4 in rounds five and six to guarantee ourselves medals. In round seven, Ding Feng's 3 against my 4 ensured that I would get a silver. The gold looked unlikely as Pupo also scored 4 to take a lead of 2 into the eighth and final round. In the final round, Pupo scored another 4 to equal the world record of 34 and claim the gold. I could only manage 2 to total 30. I was thrilled that I had won a silver medal in my debut Olympics. Ding Feng of China got the bronze.

What have been your other major achievements?

I also won five gold and a silver in the Commonwealth Games (2006 and 2010): one silver and two bronze in the Asian Games (2006 and 2010) and two silver medals in the World Shooting Championships (2009 and 2011).

How have your performances been recognized?

In 2007, I won the Arjuna Award while in 2012, I won the then Rajiv Gandhi Khel Ratna award. In 2013, I was honoured with the Padma Shri. The Army also gave me the highest promotion possible along with the Ati Vishisht Seva Medal (AVSM) for excellence in sports in 2013.

Finally, what is your message for youngsters?

I feel youngsters must be disciplined, use their heads, have a goal and remain focussed on it. Having a good guru is a must. They must never bother about setbacks. Then they will surely succeed.

Saina Nehwal - India's First World Class Woman Shuttler

Saina Nehwal, who was born on 17th March 1990 at Hisar, Haryana, is the first Indian woman badminton player to win medals in the main badminton tournaments of the world. At the 2012 London Olympics she won a bronze medal and became the first Indian badminton player to win a medal in the Olympics. In 2015, Saina attained the World No. 1 ranking becoming the first Indian woman shuttler to do so. The same year, she got a silver in the World Championships and finished runners – up in the All England tournament, becoming the first Indian woman to achieve those feats. In 2018, Saina not only became the first Indian to win singles gold medals (2010 and 2018) in the Commonwealth Games but also won a bronze medal each at the Asian Games and the Asian Championships. The Government of India conferred on Saina the Arjuna Award in 2009, the Rajiv Gandhi Khel Ratna Award in 2009-10, the Padma Shri in 2010 and the Padma Bhushan in 2016. **I spoke with Saina about her early years in badminton, her growth in the game and the finest moments in her career.**

When and how did you take to badminton?

My parents were club-level badminton players. I used to see them playing the game. My parents then put me in the badminton training course conducted in the summer of 1999. I showed interest and my parents admitted me as a regular trainee at the South SAI centre in Hyderabad in July 1999 as a day boarder initially. Later that year I became a regular. My coach was S.M. Arif sir.

When did you start training with Gopi sir and how did Gopi sir put you on the road to becoming a top class player?

When Gopi sir started his academy in 2004, I joined it. Gopi sir trained me with other trainees. He is a strict, good and concerned coach. Following his instructions and schedules, I slowly started winning tournaments and became a top level player. As I was winning tournaments, Gopi sir would give me extra attention which was very necessary during tough matches particularly in big tournaments.

What efforts and sacrifices does one have to do to be at the top?

Hard work is the crux of success. Good intent, God's Grace and good, regular meals are also necessary to be successful. Regular practice is to be followed as per the coach's instructions. Indoor gymnasium workouts, weightlifting and outdoor practice are a must to remain at the top.

What was your experience like when you were coached for three years by U Vimal Kumar at the Prakash Padukone Badminton Academy in Bengaluru?

I went to the Prakash Padukone Badminton Academy in Bengaluru towards the end of 2014. I spent three years there. Vimal Kumar sir gave me personalized coaching. During the three years I was there, Vimal Kumar sir added several facets to my game. He helped me to not only become the World No. 1 in the rankings in 2015 but also helped me win medals in the World Championship – silver in 2015 and bronze in 2017 and also a silver in the 2015 All England Championship. I am very grateful to Vimal Kumar sir, Mr. Prakash Padukone and his academy for all the help given during my stay there. I moved back to Hyderabad in the end of 2017.

How was 2018 for you?

2018 was very good as compared to 2017. In 2017, I won just one bronze and the Malaysia Masters while in 2018, I won six medals and maintained my ranking in the top ten.

My main successes in 2018 were the Commonwealth Games gold medal and a bronze each at the Asian Games and the Asian Championships.

Apart from your parents, who have supported you the most in the last year or so?

Gopi sir has been a big support. He has really helped me in a lot of tournaments but at the same time I would also like to thank my husband Kashyap. When he was injured and had time to look after me before the Asian Games, he started helping me out in some of the workouts under the guidance of Gopi sir and that changed me a lot. I feel that over the last year I am improving and I am able to challenge tough players. It is just a matter of time before I start winning tournaments again.

Please tell readers how you became India's first badminton player to win an Olympic medal.

At the London Olympics, I cruised through the group stage winning both my matches in straight games - a 21-9, 21-4 win over Sabrina Jaquet of Switzerland and a 21-4, 21-14 win over Belgium's Lianne Tan. In the round of 16, I cruised past Chinese-born Dutch sensation Yao Jie winning 21-14, 21-16.

In the quarter-final, I fought through two competitive games to defeat Tine Baun of Denmark 21-15, 22-20 to book a place in the semi-final in my first Olympics. In the semi-final, my opponent - the top seed Wang Yihan of China outplayed me to win 21-13, 21-13. In the bronze medal match on 4th August, I faced another Chinese - Wang Xin. I lost the opening game 18-21. In the second game, Wang Xin was leading 1-0 when she twisted her knee while going for an acrobatic smash from the baseline. Wang Xin retired and I earned a bronze medal - India's first Olympic medal in badminton.

Any other memorable moments in your career?

Two other memorable moments took place in 2015 when I won silver medals in the All England and World Championships. I was the first Indian woman player to achieve these feats.

Finally, who according to you is your toughest opponent?

All opponents who have defeated me in the finals of tournaments are tough opponents. However, the player I consider the most difficult to play against is Chinese Taipei's Tai Tzu-ying. She is the best.

MARY KOM – INDIA'S FIRST WOMAN OLYMPIC BOXING MEDAL WINNER

Mangte Chungneijang Mary Kom, who was born on 1st March 1983, at Kangathei, is an outstanding Indian woman boxer. She is the only woman to become World Amateur Boxing champion for a record six times, the only woman boxer to have won a medal in each one of the first seven World Championships, and the only boxer (male or female) to win eight World Championship medals. Nicknamed 'Magnificent Mary', she was the only Indian woman boxer to qualify for the 2012 Summer Olympics in London competing in the flyweight (51 kg) category and winning the

bronze medal. She has also been ranked as No.1 AIBA World Women's Ranking light flyweight category. She became the first Indian woman boxer to get a gold medal in the Asian Games in 2014 at Incheon, South Korea and is the first Indian woman boxer to win a gold at the 2018 Commonwealth Games at Gold Coast, Queensland. She is also the only boxer to become Asian Amateur Boxing Champion for a record six times. In 2016, she won the AIBA's Legends Award.

On 25th April 2016, the President of India nominated Mary Kom as a member of the Rajya Sabha, the upper house of the Indian parliament. Mary has been conferred with all the highest national awards - the Arjuna Award in 2003, the Padma Shri in 2005, the then Rajiv Gandhi Khel Ratna Award in 2009, the Padma Bhushan in 2013 and The Padma Vibhushan in 2020. **My interview with Mary Kom follows:-**

When and how did you take to Boxing?

I started my boxing career in 2000. Earlier, I was into athletics but with the introduction of women's boxing, my coach suggested that I switch to Boxing. I followed my coach's advice and switched to boxing.

Who inspired you to become a boxer and who were your coaches?

Dingko Singh, a fellow Manipuri, returned from the 1998 Bangkok Asian Games with a boxing gold medal. His success inspired many youngsters in Manipur including me to try boxing and so I took up the sport. I started my training under my first boxing coach K. Kosana Meitei. I then left my hometown to study at the Sports Academy in the state capital Imphal. Thereafter, I trained under the Manipur State boxing coach M Narjit Singh at Khuman Lampak, Imphal.

Your husband has played a great role in your career. Please tell us how.

I would say my husband Mr. Onkholer is the main person behind my success. He has been with me even before our marriage. He deals with all my professional and domestic issues and lets me concentrate fully in my training.

Mention a very memorable moment of your career saying why it was so.

My final bout during the AIBA Women's Boxing Championship on 24th November 2018 in Delhi was one of my most memorable moments. It was indeed thrilling and motivating to create history by becoming the first woman to win six World Championships in the presence of my family, my own people and thousands of cheering home fans.

Please tell readers about the bronze medal you won in the 2012 Olympics.

I had previously fought in the 46 and 48 kg categories. I shifted to the 51 kg category after the world body decided to allow women's boxing in only three weight categories eliminating the lower weight classes. This was prior to the 2012 Olympic Games.

At the 2012 AIBA Women's World Boxing Championship, I was competing not just for the championship itself but also for a place at the 2012 Summer Olympics in London, the first time women's boxing had featured as an Olympic sport. I was the only Indian woman to qualify for the boxing event. I participated in the flyweight (51 kg) division.

I was accompanied to London by my mother. My coach Charles Atkinson could not join me at the Olympic village as he did not possess an International Boxing

Association (AIBA) 3-Star Certification, which is mandatory for accreditation. The first Olympic round was held on 5th August 2012. I defeated Karolina Michalczuk of Poland 19-14. It was my toughest game in the tournament. In the quarter-final, the following day, I defeated Maroua Rahali of Tunisia with a score of 15-6. I then faced two - time world champion Nicola Adams of the United Kingdom in the semi-final on 8th August 2012 and lost the bout 6 points to 11. However, I stood third in the competition and got an Olympic bronze medal for India that day.

Why was the margin of defeat so big in the semi-final?

I was very happy to be the first Indian woman boxer to win an Olympic medal - a bronze. However, I am sad that I could not convert it into a gold. During my semi-final bout, my body somehow was not moving the way I would have liked and I felt I could not do anything. I was very confused. I never get nervous before bouts but that day I don't know what was happening to me. I can't even explain it. I was not attacking as much as I ought to have done. Maybe it was the home crowd which was cheering Nicolo. I generally do not get affected by how the crowd is behaving but probably it being the semi-final affected me. I don't think that the difference between the two of us was so much. At best, the difference could have been 2 to 3 points but certainly not 6-11. Even though my body was not moving that well, I think I hit her hard. I don't think she hit me so many punches as hers was a touch-and-go-game.

What impact did winning an Olympic medal have on your life?

Winning an Olympic bronze medal totally changed my life. It has brought me recognition and now it is much easier for me to meet people who matter and get things done.

Finally, what qualities must a person possess to be a world-level boxer?

To be a world-level boxer, one needs to be very hard working, focussed on his/her dream or goal and have patience and self-confidence. A person needs to be simple and down to earth to achieve more. I believe that one should remain humble even when one has achieved something.

Yogeshwar Dutt - A Top Class Wrestler

Yogeshwar Dutt, who was born on 2nd November 1982 at Gohana, Haryana, is an Indian wrestler from Haryana who won a bronze medal at the 2012 London Olympics. He has also won gold medals in the Asian Games and the Commonwealth Games. The Government of India conferred on him the Arjuna Award in 2009, the then Rajiv Gandhi Khel Ratna Award in 2012 and the Padma Shri in 2013. He presently runs a wrestling academy at Gohana in Haryana with the view to produce Olympic and world champions. **I spoke with Yogeshwar and asked him about his early years, his successes, Indian wrestling and his academy.**

When and how did you take to wrestling?

I took to wrestling at the age of 7. I learnt wrestling in my village from Balraj Pehelwan - a reputed wrestler. Infact, from my childhood I liked playing in the mud. I took to wrestling because I was inspired by Balraj Pehelwan and other well-known wrestlers.

Who were your coaches?

My first coach was Satbir Singh ji and it is mainly due to his guidance that I have reached the level I have attained. Later on, I received training and guidance from Ramphal Mann ji – a Dronacharya Awardee and Yashveer Dabas ji – also a Dronacharya Awardee.

What was your training for the Olympics and Asian Games like?

My training for the Olympics and Asian Games was very tough and rigorous. We trained everyday keeping in mind our strengths, tactics and match situations. We practised everyday and most often we were unable to go home for six months. During our training and competitive exposure, we were totally focussed on doing very well in the Olympics and Asian Games.

What special preparations did you do for the 2012 London Olympics?

Not having won a medal at the Beijing Olympics, I realized that my only chance of winning an Olympic medal was at London in 2012. My preparations for London began just after the Beijing Olympics. 2009 was a terrible year for me. I injured my knee and I had to undergo two operations to get back to the mat. I made a lot of changes in my attitude and technique. Then I came back strongly to win the gold in the 2010 Commonwealth Games. Two months before the Olympics, we had a three-week long camp at Colorado Springs, USA before heading to Belarus to prepare for the Olympics. During the camps, techniques, tactics and videos of likely opponents were shown and analysed. We also got quality competitive exposure.

Please tell readers about how you finished with the bronze medal in the London Olympics.

In the 2012 London Olympics, India won two wrestling medals – Sushil Kumar – a silver in the freestyle 66 kg event and myself - a bronze in the freestyle 60 kg event. At the Olympics, I lost to the Russian B Kudukhov 1-0, 2-0 and was knocked out from the pre-quarter final round. I got a chance to contest in the repechage rounds as Kudukhov reached the finals of the event. In my first repechage round, I beat Franklin Gomez of Puerto Rico with a score of 1-0, 1-0. I was lucky that I won the toss on both the occasions to earn a clinch position. In repechage round 2, I scored 7-5 to beat Masoud Esmaeilpour of Iran with an aggregate of counted points 3-1. Finally, I beat Ri Jong Myong of North Korea to clinch the bronze medal (0-1, 1-0, 6-0). I was at my best in the last round clinching it in just 1.02 minutes. I had achieved my life's dream of winning an Olympic medal.

Please tell readers about the medals you have won in the Asian Games and the Commonwealth Games.

In the 2006 Doha Asian Games, I won the bronze medal in the freestyle 60 kg event and in the 2014 Incheon Asian Games I won the gold medal in the freestyle 65 kg event. Again, in the 2010 New Delhi Commonwealth Games, I won the gold in the freestyle 60 kg event and in the 2014 Glasgow Commonwealth Games, I won the gold again in the freestyle 65 kg event.

Finally, please tell readers about your wrestling academy.

I started my wrestling academy in 2017. It is situated at Gohana in Haryana. More than 200 children are in the academy. I firmly believe that nothing can be achieved in life without discipline. The children in the academy do not keep mobile phones and are cut off from social media. I want wrestlers from my academy to become Olympic and World champions.

Sushil Kumar - India's First Individual Olympic Double Medal Winner

Please Read Along With Pages (122-125)

In the 2012 London Olympics, wrestler Sushil Kumar won the silver medal in the freestyle 66 kg event. In the process, Sushil became the first Indian sports person to win individual medals in two successive Olympics having won a bronze medal in the 2008 Beijing Olympics.

This is what Sushil Kumar had to say about the silver medal he won in the 2012 London Olympics to become the first Indian to win two individual Olympic medals in successive Olympics.

The 66 kg weight category was ideal for me. Before the London Olympics, I had two big wins. In the 2010 World Wrestling Championship in Moscow, I won the gold and became the first Indian to win a world title in wrestling. The same year, I won the gold medal in the 2010 Commonwealth Games in New Delhi. The competitions and the training camps we attended in the U.S.A. and in Belarus made me confident of doing well in the London Olympics.

In the London Olympics, I had to face Turkey's defending Olympic champion Ramazan Sahin. Sahin led 2-0 after round one but I pulled one back in the second and drew level in the final round to win by virtue of scoring last. Wins over Uzbek Iktiyor Navruzov 6-3 and Akzhurek Tanatarov of Kazakhistan 9-6 saw me become India's first Olympic finalist in wrestling.

The final was held inside three hours after my semi-final win over Kazakhstan's Tanatarov. After the semi-final, I was vomitting and was suffering from dehydration. I had also picked up a neck injury. In the final, I fought as hard as I could but the Japanese Tatsuhiro Yonemitsu was better on the day and won 4-1. True, I lost the gold medal but at least I became India's first Olympic silver medallist in Wrestling.

CHAPTER 18
SAKSHI MALIK AND P.V. SINDHU EARN INDIA MEDALS AT RIO

India sent 117 participants for 15 sports to the 2016 Rio Olympics. It was India's largest ever contingent sent to the Olympics. The increase in number of the participants was due to the return of the women's field hockey squad after 36 years, the proliferation of track and field athletes making the cut and India making its debut in Golf (new to the 2016 Games) and women's artistic gymnastics. Leander Paes was competing in a record 7th Olympics. **Abhinav Bindra was India's flag-bearer at the Opening Ceremony in his 5th consecutive Games.**

For the first time in Olympic history, both the medals won by India in the Games were won by women - a bronze by Sakshi Malik in Wrestling on 17th August followed by a silver by P V Sindhu in Badminton on 19th August. For the first time, Indian shooters failed to earn a single medal since 2004. In hockey too, both men's and women's sides failed to win a medal.

Sakshi Malik – India's First Medal Winner in Rio Olympics

Days were passing by with India not having won a medal in the 2016 Rio Olympics. It was then that Sakshi Malik, who was born on 3rd September 1992 at Rohtak, won a bronze medal in the women's freestyle 58 kg wrestling event to enable India to open its medal account at Rio on 17th August. Showing exemplary courage, determination and fighting spirit, Sakshi became the first Indian woman wrestler to win a medal in the Olympics. **I met Sakshi, who also holds a Master's degree in Physical Education, at her residence at Rohtak soon after her return from Rio and spoke with her about her career, the Olympic medal she won and wrestling in India. Her interview follows:**

Who inspired you to take to wrestling?

I was inspired by my paternal grandfather Chaudhary Badlu Ram who was a wrestler himself.

How did your parents support you in your desire to become a top class wrestler?

Girls were not thought well of if they took to wrestling as it was generally regarded as a male sport. In fact, only in 2002, we girls were allowed into the sport in Haryana. Society objected to my participating in the sport but not only was I determined, my parents too, totally backed me. I never gave up the sport despite my mother fearing that my face would spoil and some of my relatives taunting me.

When did you take to wrestling in a proper manner?

When I was 12 years old, I joined the akhara in Chotu Ram Stadium, Rohtak, where Ishwar Singh Dahiya– a 12 - time Bharat Kesari used to coach aspiring wrestlers. After a few months of training, my coach made me practise and fight with the boys because I seemed too strong for the other girls. Fortunately, I was able to make the boys struggle too. Ishwar sir, taught me a lot and was my coach till 2009 i.e. for 5 to 6 years. Mandeep then became my coach and he still helps me.

What is your normal training schedule like?

We train for about six hours in a day– both morning and evening. The training includes both physical training and practice bouts. We have to do about 500 sit-ups every day. Since our schedule is so rigorous, it has to be backed by a diet that will keep us physically strong, energetic and mentally alert.

What is your training like when the Olympics are about a year or so away?

For instance, about one and a half years before the Rio Olympics, our training and practice schedules became very rigorous. Apart from training and practising in India, we were given international exposure too. We had roughly two months training and bouts in Madrid (Spain) and Sofia (Bulgaria). We were also made to understand the tactical aspects of the game especially what should be done against which opponent.

Please tell readers about how you qualified for the Rio Olympics.

You will be surprised to know that I was not even the original choice to represent India in the Rio Olympics in the newly introduced freestyle 58 kg wrestling category. Geeta Phogat was the first choice. However, during the first Olympic qualification tournament in Ulan Bator (Mongolia) in April 2016, Geeta, slated to fight in the repechage event pulled out at the last minute citing injury. The Wrestling Federation of India was not pleased. In December 2015, I had upset Geeta in a Pro-Wrestling bout. So, for the second and final Olympic Games qualification at Istanbul, Turkey in May 2016, I participated. By God's grace, I secured the quota for the Rio Olympics winning the silver medal. In the semi-final, I defeated China's Lan Zhang.

What have been your major achievements at the international level before the Rio Olympics?

In 2010, I won a bronze medal in the Junior World Championships. In 2013, I won a bronze medal in the freestyle 63kg category in the Commonwealth Championships in Johannesburg. 2014 saw me win a silver medal in the Commonwealth Games at Glasgow in the freestyle 58 kg category. I also won a bronze medal in the freestyle 60 kg category in the 2015 Asian Championships in Doha. Finally, I qualified for the Rio Olympics by winning a silver medal in Istanbul, Turkey in May 2016.

You won India's first medal in the Rio Olympics. Describe for the benefit of readers how you won the medal.

Initially, I was defeated by Russian Valeria Koblova who made it to the final. This meant that everyone whom the Russian had beaten along the way made it to the repechage. I was determined not to let this chance of winning a medal go. I outclassed my first opponent Orkhon Purevdorj of Mongolia 12-3. An hour later, I faced my next opponent Aisuluu Tynybekova of Kyrgyzstan. Initially, I was a little tense and nervous and with barely a minute and a half to go, I was trailing 0-5. My coach Kuldeep Malik sir, then yelled out to me to get free from my opponent's grip and topple her. Following my coach's advice, I broke free and forced my rival on the mat (2-5), then once again (4-5) and went on to take a 7-5 lead. The opponent's protest at that stage was overruled and I was declared winner 8-5. I had earned India a bronze –my country's first medal at the Rio Olympics on 17th August.

What was your immediate reaction after winning the medal?

I was so thrilled and excited that I leapt into the arms of my coach. He lifted me on his shoulders and did a victory lap with myself draped in the Indian tri-colour.

What qualities does one need to possess to become a top level wrestler?

Apart from strength which has to combine with tactical intelligence, a wrestler in order to become top class needs to be dedicated and have a proper diet and take sufficient rest.

What must India do to produce a lot of top class wrestlers?

Wrestling must be encouraged at the grassroots level. There must be residential academies where the trainees are carefully selected and looked after properly. Dedicated coaches are a must so that proper care is taken regarding the stay, training, diet and mental health of the trainees.

Finally, what is your message for the girls of our country?

The country must realise that we girls are no less than the boys in any field. We girls can achieve anything if we get the opportunities and encouragement. I hope the girls get inspired and reach greater heights in the future.

P.V. SINDHU – INDIAN BADMINTON GREAT

Pusarla Venkata Sindhu, who was born on 5th July 1995 at Hyderabad, became the first Indian badminton player to win an Olympic silver medal in the 2016 Rio Olympics. She is the first Indian badminton player to win the World Badminton Championship. She achieved this feat on 25th August 2019 at Basel, Switzerland.

Sindhu's record in the World Badminton Championships is a total of 5 medals (2 bronze, 2 silver and 1 gold) equalling the record of China's Zhang Ning who was the first to win five medals in the World Badminton Championships. In 2018, Sindhu won the BWF World Tour finals. She is a two-time Asian Games medallist – bronze in 2014 and silver in 2018 while in the Commonwealth Games, Sindhu has also won two medals – a bronze in 2014 and a silver in 2018. The Government of India conferred on her the Arjuna Award in 2013, the Padma Shri in 2015, the Rajiv Gandhi Khel Ratna Award in 2016 and the Padma Bhushan in 2020. **I spoke with Sindhu and asked her about the role of her parents, Gopi sir and others and also about the best moments in her badminton career.**

Please tell readers about your parents and their contribution to your success.

My father P.V. Ramana and my mother P.Vijaya were national level volleyball players. My father was a member of the Indian volleyball team that won a bronze medal in the 1986 Seoul Asian Games. He was conferred the Arjuna Award in 2000. My parents laid the foundation for me and are the pillars of my success. Without their sacrifices, I do not think I could have achieved what I have.

Despite your parents being volleyball players what made you take up badminton?

In 2001, Gopi sir or rather Pullela Gopichand won the All England Open Badminton Championships and that inspired me to take to the game.

How and when did you first start learning the game?

My father was with the Railways. So, I first learned the basics of the sports from Mehboob Ali at the badminton courts of the Indian Railway Institute of Signal Engineering and Telecommunications in Secunderabad. Soon after, I joined Pullela Gopichand's Badminton Academy. Thanks to my parents – my father in particular, I used to be in time for the coaching after travelling a distance of 56 km from my residence.

What is the role Gopi sir has played in your career?

Gopi sir has played an integral part in my career. Not only has he been my coach from the time I was very young, he has also been a mentor to me. Apart from correcting any errors that might have crept into my game, he has also greatly helped me as a mentor. This is reflected by my body language and confidence on the court. Gopi sir keeps pushing me to reach greater heights without ever putting pressure on me. So keen is he on my success that a couple of weeks before the Rio Olympics in order to keep me fit, he restricted the sweet curd in my diet. I have also made it a habit of keeping away from my mobile before and during competitions. His presence in this year's World Badminton Championship was very reassuring for me.

Apart from your parents and Gopi sir, two others played a part in your becoming the World Champion – Korean coach Kim Ji-hyun and strength trainer Srikanth Verma. Please tell readers about how they contributed to your big success.

The Korean coach Kim Ji-hyun has been with me for a couple of months. Her one - to - one sessions with me proved very helpful. She helped me to work on my defence and also encouraged me to be more aggressive from the start so as to put pressure on the opponent. Srikanth Verma contributed hugely in his own way. He identified the weak areas in my body which affected my front court moment and worked on them. In the last few days he worked on strengthening my body mass. Srikanth was the person who helped me to play the 110-minute 2017 World Championship final at a very intense level.

Which early win of yours do you still cherish to date?

Without doubt it was my 21-19, 9-21, 21-16 forty-five minute win over the newly crowned Olympic champion and then world no. 3 Li Xuerui of China in the quarter-final of the China Masters Super Series at Changzuou in 2012. Being 17 years of age, I was really delighted to defeat Li as she was in great form that year. It was an amazing feeling. I began the third game well and succeeded in maintaining that momentum.

What have been the two finest and most memorable moments of your career to date?

My finest and happiest moment in my career to date has to be my becoming the World Champion this year – the first Indian to achieve this distinction. I was fortunately at my best in the final and so Okuhara could neither play her game nor react. In 38 minutes, I won 21-7, 21-7. In the 2017 final, I had lost to Okuhara 21-19, 20-22, 20-22 in a pulsating encounter which lasted an hour and 50 minutes. After winning silvers in 2017 and 2018, I was thrilled and relieved to win the gold this year. I felt great seeing our national flag going up and hearing our national anthem being played. It was the best gift I could give my mother on her birthday.

The second moment has to be the 2016 Rio Olympics where I won a historic silver medal.

Please tell readers in detail about the Olympic silver medal you won at the 2016 Rio Olympics.

In my first Olympics at Rio, I was drawn at the group-stage with Michelle Li of Canada and Hungary's

Laura Sarosi. I easily defeated Sarosi 21-8, 21-9 and then recovered after being a game down to defeat Li 19-21, 21-15, 21-17 to go through to the last 16. I then found my form. I first brushed aside Chinese Taipei's Tai Tzu-ying 21-13, 21-15 and then got the better of Wang Yihan of China 22-20, 21-19 to reach the semi-final. In the semi-final, I defeated Japan's Nozomi Okuhara 21-19, 21-10 to become India's first Olympic badminton finalist. In a hard-fought final on 19th August, I lost to two-time world champion Spain's Carolina Marin 21-19, 12-21, 15-21 to finish runner-up and take the silver medal. At 21 years - 1 month - 14 days, I became the youngest Indian to win an Olympic medal. I also became the first Indian woman to win a silver medal in the Olympics.

Finally, any advice for schools regarding the importance of sports.

Sports should be made compulsory in schools. This is not because children have to become champions, but because I feel exercise is very important for everyone. It is not always about studies. Children also need to have clear and healthy minds.

CHAPTER 19

NEERAJ CHOPRA'S GOLD IN TOKYO HELPS INDIA BETTER ITS LONDON MEDAL AGGREGATE

India bettered its aggregate of six medals in the 2012 London Olympics due to the gold medal won by javelin thrower Neeraj Chopra on 7th August. Chopra's gold was India's first medal in Athletics since India's independence. India finished with 7 medals (1 gold, 2 silver and 4 bronze). The 2020 Tokyo Olympics, originally scheduled to take place from 24th July to 9th August 2020, was postponed to 23rd July to 8th August 2021 due to the COVID 19 pandemic. India sent its largest contingent of 126 competitors to these Games. **India's flag-bearers at the Opening Ceremony were M C Mary Kom, Olympic boxing bronze medallist and the men's hockey team's captain Manpreet Singh.**

Weightlifter Saikhom Mirabai Chanu got India its first medal at Tokyo when she won a silver medal in the women's 49 kg event on 24th July - India's first day at the competition. On 1st August, P V Sindhu, who had won a silver medal in the Badminton ladies singles event in the 2016 Rio Olympics, won for India its second medal - a bronze. Sindhu became the first Indian woman and second Indian, after wrestler Sushil Kumar (bronze in 2008 and silver in 2012) to achieve the distinction of winning a medal in two successive Olympics. Three days later on 4th August, Lovlina Borgohain won a bronze medal in the women's welterweight event in Boxing. The following day, India won two medals - a bronze in the men's hockey team event and wrestler Ravi Kumar Dahiya's silver in the men's freestyle 57 kg event. The hockey medal was significant as it was India's first medal in Olympic hockey since the 1980 Moscow Olympics. 7th August was a great day for Indian sports. Bajrang Punia first won a bronze medal in wrestling in the men's freestyle 65 kg event. Bajrang's success was followed by an outstanding performance by javelin thrower Neeraj Chopra who left all his competitors behind to easily win the gold medal. Neeraj Chopra's gold medal was India's second individual gold medal in the Olympics - the first one was won by shooter Abhinav Bindra in the 10 m air rifle event at the 2008 Beijing Olympics. Neeraj Chopra's medal was India's first Olympic medal in Athletics since independence.

In addition to the performances of these medal winners, there were other notable performances. But the two which stood out were first of all, the unheralded women's hockey team which made it to the semi-final while participating in the competition for only the third time. The team was unlucky to lose to Great Britain in the bronze medal play-off and finish fourth. The other great performance was that of young golfer Aditi Ashok who finished fourth despite being in second position till the end of the third round. Aditi, who had finished 41st in the 2016 Rio Olympics, not only played superb golf but also made the world take note of Indian Golf- in particular women's golf. The biggest disappointment was our shooters returning without a medal for the second successive Olympics.

Saikhom Mirabai Chanu – A Silver Lining For Indian Weightlifting

Saikhom Mirabai Chanu is India's second Olympic medal winner in Weightlifting but the first to win an Olympic silver medal. Chanu, who was born on 8th August 1994 in Nongpok, Kakching,

Imphal, Manipur, achieved this feat on 24th July when she stood second in the women's 49 kg weightlifting event. Her medal was India's first in the 2020 Tokyo Olympics.

Chanu's obsession for being neat and tidy almost made her take up archery. "All my brothers and cousins played football and they would come back home dirty after a day's play. I wanted to play a sport which was neat and clean. At first, I wished to be an archer as archers are neat, clean and stylish, " said Chanu.

As a 13-year - old from a low-income family living around 20 km from Manipur's capital Imphal, Chanu decided early in her life that she would make it big as a sportsperson. In the quest to find a sports facility and a mentor, she travelled with a cousin to the Sports Authority of India (SAI) Centre at Khuman Lampak in Imphal in early 2008. However, she did not find any training for archery that day. Around that time, she saw clippings of the legendary Manipuri weightlifter Kunjarani Devi, which inspired her to the core. So, after a few days, she went to the weightlifting training centre and fortunately met former international weightlifter and coach Anita Chanu, who initiated the youngster to the sport.

Chanu was a strong and determined girl. At that age, she could lift more firewood than her elder brother. She would not only cut wood at the nearby hills and bring them by herself but also fetch water in milk powder cans from ponds close by. Chanu toiled hard at that young age so that she could adjust her training to her school schedule. This was because she had to reach the training centre every day at 6 am and change the bus twice from her village on a 22 km journey.

In time, thanks to the hard work she put in and the training she received, Chanu made rapid strides in weightlifting. She lifted 170 kg to win a silver in the 2014

Commonwealth Games in Glasgow but put up a disappointing show in the Rio Olympics. At the Rio Olympics in 2016, Chanu fell short of the expected standards. She failed in her first two lifts in snatch and just about made her third attempt. In the clean and jerk, Chanu did not have a single clean lift.

"Since the Rio Olympics, I have tried to balance my nutrition and diet and focussed both on the physical and mental aspects of my training. I have worked hard on my technique, especially in snatch. I changed my training methods and with the work I have put in, my snatch is at par with my clean and jerk, " said Chanu. Chanu further added, "Every one helped me to remain focussed and look forward to the upcoming competitions and keep working hard. They made me realize that I was young and had a long career ahead."

Chanu has made a great comeback since her Rio debacle. She first silenced her detractors by winning the gold in the 48 kg event in the 2017 World Championships held at Anaheim in California and in the Gold Coast Commonwealth Games a year later. Besides, she also overcame an unspecified back problem which marred her progress in 2018. It was then she changed her weight category to 49 kg. She continued to compete in different events till the pandemic - induced break.

However, her body was full of pain due to dreadful injuries. In 2020, her coach Vijay Sharma - the biggest influence on Chanu's career and successes - decided to take Chanu to St. Louis, USA to train and recover under Dr Aaron Horschig, a former weightlifter who is one of the most eminent physiotherapists in the United States of America, having worked with top-level baseballers, footballers and Olympic weightlifters. Horschig showed the path of recovery to Chanu and this was reflected in her performance at the Asian Championship in 2020, where she created the erstwhile world record. Chanu became the first Indian to catch up with the Chinese weightlifters, defeating the gold medallist Hou Zhihui in clean and jerk. Chanu qualified for the Tokyo Olympics by getting a bronze medal in the 2020 Asian Championship in Tashkent. She also created a world record in Tashkent lifting 119 kg in the clean and jerk.

On 24th July, in the final of the 49 kg weightlifting event at the Tokyo Olympics, Chanu won the silver medal lifting a total of 202 kg - 87 kg in snatch and 115 kg in clean and jerk. She successfully lifted 84kg and 87 kg in the first two attempts in the snatch category but failed in her final attempt in which she targetted 89 kg. In the clean and jerk section, Chanu lifted 110 kg and 115 kg in her first two attempts. However, in her final attempt, she could not lift the required 117 kg. Chanu had assured herself of a silver medal. The gold medal was won by China's Hou Zhihui (210 kg). **My questions to Chanu along with her answers follow:**

How can families help in youngsters taking to sports?

Families must encourage their children - boys and girls to take to sports. Children must be allowed to take up any game of their choice. Only after they play a game, the scouts will spot their talent and send them to specialist coaches for training. Parents must realize that their children can make successful careers out of sports.

Finally, what has to be done to get better results from our sports persons?

Apart from quality training and competitive exposure, our sports persons need to be supported morally and emotionally 365 days each year and not every four years. There are a lot of struggles (injuries, rehab, poor form) in a sports person's life. The players need to be supported in times of struggle too. Consolation and sympathy are no substitutes for constant moral and emotional support.

For her services to weightlifting, the Government of India conferred on Chanu the Padma Shri in 2018 and the then Rajiv Gandhi Khel Ratna Award for 2018.

P. V. Sindhu - The First Indian Woman To Win Medals In Successive Olympics

Please Read Along With Pages (149-153)

P. V. Sindhu, the silver medallist in the Rio Olympics, participated in the Tokyo Olympics with the intention getting another Olympic medal - preferably a gold. Sindhu finished with a bronze at Tokyo as in the semi-final, she lost to Tai Tzu-ying of Chinese Taipei 18-21, 12-21. **Now read on to know how she prepared for the Tokyo Olympics and what her performance was like.**

For the Tokyo Olympics, Sindhu had a new coach in Park Tae Sang of South Korea. Park had been with Sindhu since late 2019. He had taken over as Sindhu's coach from another South Korean Kim Ji - Hyun who had helped Sindhu win the BWF World Championship at Basel in 2019. According to Sindhu, "The personal attention I am getting from Park has been very helpful in keeping me prepared for my pressure situations on court. His personal attention has helped me a lot. Park understands what is going on in my mind. When I am under pressure or in a difficult situation, he lets me think for myself. The eye-to-eye coordination with him works perfectly. He knows when to intervene and his reading of my opponents is fantastic. When events were cancelled, he created tricky match situations for me in training, "

In the group stage of the Tokyo Olympics, Sindhu first defeated Israel's Ksenia Polikarpova 21-7, 21-10 on 25th July and in the next match on 28th July, she scored a 21-9, 21-16 win over Hong Kong's Cheung Ngan Yi. The following day, in the pre- quarter-final, Sindhu played with consistency to defeat Denmark's Mia Blichfeldt 21-15, 21-13. Blichfeldt had defeated Sindhu in January 2021 in the first round of the Thailand Open.

On 30th July, Sindhu met local star and higher seeded Akane Yamaguchi in the quarter-final. Yamaguchi tried everything she could but Sindhu was confident and consistent, She attacked whenever needed. Sindhu displayed great control all round to win 21-13, 22-20. The second game was hard-fought.

In the semi-final on 31st July, Sindhu faced World No. 1 Tai Tzu -ying of Chinese Taipei. In the first game, Sindhu was either in the lead or level up to 17/18. After that, Tai got two or three quick points and won the game. Had those points gone Sindhu's way, the outcome of the match would have been different as winning the first game gives a psychological advantage. In the second game, Tai, who is one of the most skillful players in the world, started going for her strokes. Sindhu also made some mistakes which enabled Tai to win 21-18, 21-12 and make it to the final.

Sindhu met He Bing Jiao of China on 1st August in the bronze medal match. Sindhu was at her aggressive best totally outplaying her opponent 21-13, 21-15. In this match, Sindhu was determined, consistent and pro-active. To quote Sindhu, " After the semi-final match, I was disappointed but my coach told me that there is a lot of difference between a bronze medal and a fourth place. So I was determined to win even though my opponent He Bing Jiao had defeated me six times in our last nine encounters, "

By winning the bronze medal, Sindhu became the first Indian woman to win medals in successive Olympics. She is also the second Indian to achieve this distinction after wrestler Sushil Kumar.

LOVLINA BORGOHAIN - INDIAN BOXING'S SAVING GRACE IN TOKYO

On 4th August, boxer Lovlina Borgohain, who was born on 2nd October 1997 in village Baramukhiya, Golaghat district of Assam, became India's lone boxing medal winner in the Tokyo Olympics and the country's third Olympic medal winner in Boxing. Lovlina got a bronze after making it to the semi-final of the welterweight category where she was defeated by World No.1 and top-seeded Busenaz Surmeneli of Turkey 0-5. About her defeat at the hands of Surmeneli, Lovlina said, " I could not apply the strategy I had made. Surmeneli was undoubtedly physically stronger than me but not so much better technically. I have now realized my shortcomings."

Earlier on 27th July, Lovlina won her round of 16 bout against Nadine Apetz of Germany 3-2 following it up on 30th July with a most creditable 4-1 win over Nien- Chin Chen of Chinese Taipei, the fourth seed and a former world champion in the quarter-final. Lovlina used her speed and height effectively and intelligently to outsmart her tough and strong punching opponent.

Now here are some details about Lovlina's life and career till the Tokyo Olympics. Lovlina's parents are Tiken and Mamoni Borgohain. She has two elder twin sisters Licha and Lima. The father struggled financially with the family facing very difficult times but despite all that, the mother would constantly motivate the children to aim big. The father loved sports and so encouraged the children to play games. Lovlina's elder sisters took part in kickboxing and competed at the national level. They did not pursue it beyond that.

Right from the beginning, it was Lovlina's aim to make it to the Olympics and perform well. So, she was keen to shift to boxing. The Sports Authority of India held boxing trials at her school - Barpathar Girls High School. Lovlina attended the trials and was noticed and selected by renowned coach Padum Bora, who began training her in 2012. After the trials, she joined the Netaji Subhas Regional Centre in Guwahati for specialized training. From Guwahati she shifted to Bhopal to be coached by Shiv Singh for more scientific and top-level coaching and training.

Lovlina had a number of good performances in 2017 and 2018 at the international level. In June 2017, she won the bronze medal at the President's Cup in Astana and in November the same year she won the bronze medal at the Asian Boxing Championships in Ho Chi Minh City, Vietnam. Her gold medal in the welterweight category in the inaugural Indian Open held in February 2018 provided her with her career's biggest break - being selected to participate in the welterweight boxing category at the 2018 Gold Coast Commonwealth Games. At the Commonwealth Games, she lost to Sandy Ryan from Great Britain in the quarter-finals. Sandy Ryan went on to win the gold in that category. The Games made Lovlina a better boxer as she realized how much more she had to do to become a top-level boxer. In June 2018, Lovlina won a silver medal at the Ulaanbaatar Cup in

Mongolia and a bronze medal in September that year in the 13th International Silesian Championship in Gliwice, Poland. In November 2018, Lovlina represented India for the first time at the AIBA Women's World Boxing Championships in New Delhi. She won a bronze medal in the welterweight category.

In October 2019, Lovlina was defeated 2-3 by China's Yang Liu in the semi-final of the welterweight category and had to settle for a bronze in her second Women's World Boxing Championships in Ulan-Ude, Russia. Then, in March 2020, Lovlina secured her berth for the 2020 Tokyo Olympics in the welterweight category with a 5-0 win over Maftunakhon Melieva of Uzbekistan in the 2020 Asia and Oceania Boxing Olympic Qualification tournament. She then lost to Gu Hong of China in a unanimous 0-5 verdict to sign off with a bronze medal.

For her great contribution to Indian boxing, Lovlina was conferred the Arjuna Award in 2020 and the Dhyan Chand Khel Ratna Award in 2021.

Indian Men's Hockey Team's First Olympic Medal Since 1980

The Indian men's hockey team captained by midfielder Manpreet Singh - a three-time Olympian and coached by Australian Graham Reid earned an Olympic medal (a bronze) at Tokyo- the first hockey medal since the 1980 Moscow Olympics. The side played competitive hockey throughout except against Australia to win the bronze medal by defeating Germany 5-4 in the bronze medal play-off on 5th August.

Manpreet Singh
India's Medal Winning Captain

Manpreet Singh Sandhu, who was born on 26th June 1992 in Mithapur village on the outskirts of Jalandhar city, is a very experienced player who is one of the best midfielders in international hockey.

This star midfielder first represented India in 2011 at the age of 19. In the ten years of international hockey he has played, Manpreet has been part of the gold and silver medal-winning teams in the Incheon Asian Games and the Glasgow Commonwealth Games respectively in 2014. He then captained the Asia Cup winning side at Dhaka in 2017 and the silver medal-winning Champions Trophy side in 2018 at Breda. The Tokyo Olympics medal was another feather in his cap.

Manpreet again captained the Indian team that won a silver medal in the 2022 Commonwealth Games in Birmingham. He was also a member of the team which won the gold medal at the Hangzhou Asian Games.

Manpreet was conferred the Arjuna Award in 2018 and in 2019, he was named Men's FIH Player of the Year.

Skipper Manpreet's answers to the questions put by me follow:

How helpful was the time spent together by the team in the lockdown?

From the human angle, we shared a lot of personal things with each other. We became closer to each other and lived like a family. We always got positive vibes from each other. This closeness and family feeling contributed a lot to our team doing well. From the tactical side, we went back to the drawing board to refresh ourselves. We discussed and analysed with each other the strengths and weaknesses of other teams and their players. The understanding between each one of us became great.

How significant was the team's tour to Argentina before the Tokyo Olympics?

Argentina, the 2016 Rio Olympics champions, are a very difficult team to play against. They are very physical. Their one-to-one marking is very difficult to break as they hardly give you any breathing space. The thing that impressed me most on the tour was how we fought back despite conceding early goals. The greatest takeaway for me was that the players were ready to fight till the end.

How did the team recover from the 1-7 defeat at the hands of Australia in the second pool match?

The 1-7 defeat at the hands of Australia was very disappointing. But, when we analyzed the match and checked the data, we realized that it was Australia's lucky day. Everything they threw at us, even a push, went in. But, it was not for us. Data on circle penetrations pointed to a 3-2 or 2-2 kind of a score. So, we decided that we would put in our 100 percent every time and not lose any other match. After that game, we only lost to Belgium in the semi-final.

Please take us through the feelings of the players during the bronze medal match.

Germany is considered to have one of the best defences in the world. Scoring against them is difficult. We were down 1-3 but we did not give up. We kept telling ourselves that these 60 minutes will not come back. At any cost, we did not want to experience the regret of not winning a medal. Hence our fightback from 1-3 to 5-3 and the effort we put in at the end to ensure Germany did not get the equalizer after they had made it 4-5. We had also worked a lot on fixing our last- minute errors.

Finally, what does Indian hockey (men's and women's) need to do to take its successes in the Tokyo Olympics forward?

Both the Indian men's and women's hockey players are happy though not fully satisfied with our performances in the Tokyo Olympics. Both our teams are clearly among the best in the world. For us, to take these successes forward, we need to carry on working hard, keep our mindset strong believing that we can defeat any opposition and finally, never under-estimating any team we play.

Indian Team: Standing (L to R) Rupinder Pal Singh, Surender Kumar, Manpreet Singh (Captain), Gurjant Singh, Harmanpreet Singh, P. R. Sreejesh, Amit Rohidas, Lalit Kumar Upadhyay, Birendra Lakra,

Sitting (L to R) Dilpreet Singh, Hardik Singh, Simranjeet Singh, Mandeep Singh, Varun Kumar, Shamsher Singh, Vivek Sagar Prasad, Sumit Walmiki, Nilakanta Sharma.

At Tokyo, there were two pools comprising of six teams each. India was placed in Pool A along with Australia, Argentina, the defending champions, Spain, New Zealand and hosts Japan. The top four teams of each pool qualified for the quarter-final stage.

On 24th July, India met New Zealand in its first match. It was a well-fought game with India winning 3-2. New Zealand's Kane Russell converted a penalty corner to put his side 1-0 ahead in the 6th minute of play. Four minutes later, India restored parity when Rupinder Pal converted a penalty stroke. Harmanpreet with two goals in the 26th and 33rd minutes put India 3-1 ahead. New Zealand reduced the lead in the 43rd minute through a goal by Stephen Jenness. In the dying minutes of the game, it was goalkeeper Sreejesh's brilliance that helped India win 3-2.

The following day, India met Australia, the strongest team in Pool A. Australia, who displayed craft and class trounced India 7-1. This was India's biggest defeat in Olympic hockey. The previous one was the 1-6 defeat at the hands of Australia again in the 1976 Montreal Olympics when nearly all the players were new to astro-turf. In the 10th minute of play, Daniel Beale put Australia 1-0 ahead. Jeremy Hayward doubled the lead in the 21st minute by converting a penalty corner. Australia added two more goals in the span of five minutes through Andrew Flynn Ogilvie and Joshua Beltz in the 23rd and 26th minutes respectively. India's Dilpreet reduced the deficit in the 34th minute but it was a little too late. Australia scored three more times through Blake Govers (40th and 42nd minutes) and Tim Brand (51st minute) to win 7-1.

After its crushing defeat vs Australia, India played more purposeful hockey to defeat Spain 3-0 on 27th July. India was at its best in the first quarter of the match. In the 14th minute, India took the lead through Simranjeet who capitalized on a pass from Amit Rohidas. A minute later, Rupinder Pal converted a penalty stroke. Spain was dominant in the second and third quarters but they could not score. India made it 3-0 in the 51st minute when Rupinder Pal scored through a low penalty corner conversion.

India's next match was on 29th July against Argentina, the defending champions. It was a crucial match as the result of the game would decide the second spot in the pool. India played good attacking hockey which put a lot of pressure on Argentina. It was only in the 43rd minute, Varun Kumar, playing his first match in Tokyo, gave India the lead by converting a penalty corner. Argentina equalized in the 48th minute through Maico Casella. With a couple of minutes to go for the end of the game, Argentina's defence suddenly wilted under pressure. India scored two goals in this period through Vivek Sagar Prasad in the 58th minute and Harmanpreet off a penalty corner conversion in the 59th minute. India finished 3-1 winners.

In the final pool match on 30th July, India continued its winning streak defeating Japan, the hosts and 2018 Asian Games winners, 5-3. India's scorers were Harmanpreet (13th minute), Gurjant (17th and 56th minutes), Shamsher Singh (34th minute) and Nilakanta Sharma (51st minute) while Japan's scorers were Kenta Tanaka (19th minute), Kota Watanabe (33rd minute) and Kazuma Murata (59th minute).

India, who finished second in its pool, met Great Britain, who finished third in Pool B, in the quarter-final on 2nd August. India played quite well to win 3-1. Dilpreet got India an early lead in the 7th minute. Gurjant increased the lead when he scored in the 16th minute. At the end of the second quarter, India led 2-0. In the dying minutes of the third quarter, Sam Ward reduced the deficit for Great Britain. In the final quarter, Great Britain tried hard but could not score. Then, in the 57th minute of play, Hardik scored a stunning goal to ensure India reach the semi-finals with a 3-1 win.

On 3rd August, India met Belgium, the Pool B toppers and world champions, in the semi-final. Both teams fought evenly and went into the last quarter with the score 2-2. Belgium took the lead in the 2nd minute of the start of the game when Loick Fanny Luypaert converted a penalty corner. Five minutes later, India equalized when Harmanpreet scored with a low drive. The next minute India went into the lead when Mandeep slapped a reverse hit past the Belgium goalie after receiving a brilliant cross pass from Amit Rohidas. In the 19th minute of play, Belgium's penalty corner specialist Alexander Hendrickx restored parity converting a penalty corner. In thc final stages of the game, India's skipper Manpreet Singh got a green card and India was reduced to ten men. Belgium continued to put pressure on the Indian goal to score three more goals - two by Hendrickx in the 49th and 53rd minutes (a hat-trick) and the final one by John - John Dohmen in the 60th minute. Belgium won 5-2 at the end to enter the final.

In the bronze medal play-off against Germany on 5th August, Germany started off playing very fast and attacking hockey which resulted in Timur Oruz scoring his side's first goal in the second minute of the match. India equalized in the 17th minute through Simranjeet who capitalized on a wonderful pass from Nilakanta Sharma. In the 24th minute, Germany went into the lead through Niklas Wellen. Germany then further increased its lead in the very next minute when Benedikt Fürk scored. India then showed remarkable fighting spirit from 1-3 down. In the 27th minute, Hardik scored capitalizing on a rebound caused by Rupinder Pal's flick. Harmanpreet and Rupinder Pal then converted two penalty corners in the 29th and 31st minutes respectively to put India ahead 4-3. Then, Simranjeet scored in the 34th minute to make the score 5-3 in India's favour. The final quarter was tense with Germany scoring off a penalty corner in the 48th minute by Lukas Windfeder. Germany kept on pushing for goals but the Indian defence held firm. So, India got a bronze medal in hockey - its first Olympic medal in the sport since the 1980 Olympics.

Results:

Pool A - beat New Zealand 3-2 (Rupinder Pal Singh 1, Harmanpreet Singh 2)

lost to Australia 1-7 (Dilpreet Singh 1)

beat Spain 3-0 (Simranjeet Singh 1, Rupinder Pal Singh 2)

beat Argentina 3-1 (Varun Kumar 1, Vivek Sagar Prasad 1, Harmanpreet Singh 1)

beat Japan 5-3 (Harmanpreet Singh 1, Gurjant 2, Shamsher Singh 1, Nilakanta Sharma 1)

Quarter-final - beat Great Britain 3-1 (Dilpreet Singh 1, Gurjant Singh 1, Hardik Singh 1)

Semi-final - lost to Belgium 2-5 (Harmanpreet Singh 1, Mandeep Singh 1)

Bronze medal play-off - beat Germany 5-4 (Simranjeet Singh 2, Hardik Singh 1, Harmanpreet Singh 1, Rupinder Pal Singh 1)

Final Positions - Belgium 1, Australia 2, India 3, Germany 4, Great Britain 5, the Netherlands 6, Argentina 7, Spain 8, New Zealand 9, South Africa 10, Japan 11, Canada 12.

Ravi Kumar Dahiya - Second Indian Wrestler To Win Olympic Silver

Ravi Kumar Dahiya, who was born on 12th December 1997 in Nahri, Sonepat district, became India's fifth wrestler to win an Olympic medal (India's sixth medal as Sushil Kumar had won two medals) when he lost 4-7 in the final to the reigning world champion Zavur Uguev representing Russian Olympic Committee (ROC) in the freestyle 57 kg event on 5th August. After Sushil Kumar, he became the second Indian wrestler to win an Olympic silver medal.

The 23- year-old wrestler started his Tokyo Olympic campaign on 4th August winning his first two bouts by 'technical superiority' where a bout is stopped because one wrestler has taken a ten-point lead over the other. Ravi Dahiya first got the better of Colombia's Tigreros Urbano 13-2 to reach the quarter-finals. He then stormed into the semi-finals defeating Bulgaria's Georgi Valentinov Vangelov 14-4. Ravi Dahiya exhibited pure brute strength and agility in this match.

In the semi-final on 4th August, Ravi Dahiya displayed great recovery skills fighting back to win from an almost hopeless situation. His opponent in the semi-final was Nurislam Sanayev of Kazakhstan, a two-time world championship medallist. With the contest entering the final stages, Ravi Dahiya was trailing 2-9. It was then he summoned everything in his command to turn the tables on his opponent in a dramatic fashion. He clinched the issue by 'pinfall', even though the score showed the Kazakh leading 9-7. In the final minute of the contest, Ravi Dahiya started reducing the deficit by first pushing Sanayev 'out of bounds' (off the mat) and then tripping him to earn three points. With the score-line still favouring the Kazakh at 9-5, Ravi Dahiya went for the single- drive leg attack and scored a two-point takedown before converting it to a pin, where he snapped Sanayev's shoulders and kept them fixed to the mat to be declared winner 'by fall'. So, Ravi Dahiya became, after Sushil Kumar, India's second Olympic wrestling finalist.

The next day, Ravi Dahiya met Zavur Uguev, the two-time world champion, in the final. Uguev was swift with his counters and strong in defence and so finished a 7-4 winner. Ravi Dahiya had to be content with a silver medal. Uguev took a 2-0 lead through step-outs. Ravi Dahiya brought him down to parity but Uguev scored another two points with a takedown even as Ravi Dahiya did well to avoid getting tangled. In the second period, with Uguev leading 4-2, Ravi Dahiya stepped up the attack but Uguev scored another three points with a fast counter. With one-and-a-half minutes remaining, a takedown gave Ravi Dahiya two more points but that was all he could add to his tally. So, Ravi Dahiya ended up losing 4-7. About his defeat, Ravi Dahiya had this to say, "Uguev's style was very good. He wrestled very smartly. I just could not find a way to play my game. I had prepared keeping him in mind for this Olympics. However, my defeat shows that there is still a lot of work to be done."

Now here is some information about Ravi Dahiya and his achievements till the Tokyo Olympics. Ravi's father, Rakesh, was a farmer who worked on rented paddy fields. Braving all odds, Ravi started wrestling at the age of six with minimal facilities available in the village. He first practised in an akhada (wrestling pit) on soil and then, at the age of ten, went to the Chhatrasal Stadium in Delhi to be trained by Satpal ji. Later, Ravi's personal coach Kamal Malikov of Russia played a role in his successes in international competitions and the Tokyo Olympics. Rakesh was so keen about his son Ravi's success as a wrestler that he would travel every day from Nahri to the stadium for more than a decade to deliver milk and fruits, which were part of his son's wrestling diet.

Ravi Dahiya won the silver medal in the freestyle 55 kg category at the 2015 Junior World Wrestling Championships in Salvador de Bahia. He picked up an injury in 2017 which kept him out of action for more than a year. In his comeback year, he won the silver medal in the freestyle 57 kg category at the 2018 World Under-23 Wrestling Championships in Bucharest. In his World Championships debut in 2019 at Nur-Sultan, Kazakhstan, Ravi Dahiya defeated the European champion Arsen Harutyunyan in the round of 16 and the 2017 world champion Yuki Takahashi in the quarter-final to earn one of the quota places for the Tokyo Olympics. In the semi-final, he lost to the eventual gold medallist Zavur Uguev and finished with a bronze medal in the freestyle 57 kg event. Ravi Dahiya also bagged the gold in the freestyle 57 kg event at the 2020 and 2021 Asian Wrestling Championships in New Delhi and Almaty respectively.

For his services to wrestling, Ravi was conferred the Major Dhyan Chand Khel Ratna Award for 2021.

Bajrang Punia Bags India's Second Wrestling Medal - A Bronze

Bajrang Punia, who was born on 26th February 1994 in Khudan village, Jhajjar, Haryana, finished with a bronze medal on 7th August when he outclassed Kazakhstan's Daulat Niyazbekov 8-0 to win the freestyle 65 kg bronze medal bout. Removing the strapping on his right knee, Bajrang, unlike the previous day, was unfettered. He showed his class and stamped his authority over the two-time world championship medal winner. About removing the strapping, Bajrang said, "For me winning the Olympic medal was more important than the injury and so I removed the strapping." Bajrang's medal was India's second wrestling medal of the Olympics after Ravi Kumar Dahiya's silver. It was also the seventh wrestling medal to be won by an Indian in the Olympics.

Earlier on 6th August, Bajrang started his campaign with a heavily-strapped injured right knee. The knee had been injured at Moscow's Ali Aliyev invitational event on 25th June. Bajrang had gone to Moscow to train for the Olympics and get competitive exposure. The injury had kept him off the mat for nearly two weeks. In his first three bouts, Bajrang's knee was strapped.

In his first bout on 6th August, Bajrang struggled to close out the bout against Kyrgyzstan's Ernazar Akmataliev after leading 3-1 with little time left. It was a gripping contest with Akmataliev looking to get hold of Bajrang's injured knee but Bajrang did just enough to stave off the challenge. However, Akmataliev levelled the score at 3-3 with two late ' out of bounds' and looked for a last-gasp takedown. But Bajrang survived owing to his highest scoring move in the first period - a two-point takedown compared to Akmataliev's single-point pushouts - to win and enter the quarter-finals. The final score was 3-3.

In the quarter-final against Morteza Ghiasi Cheka of Iran, Bajrang was left defending his right knee from the beginning of the bout as his opponent went on the offensive to effect a takedown. Bajrang knew that more than brawn, it would take tactical acumen to get the better of the relentless attacks of his opponent. So, Bajrang waited for the opening to arrive and, with one swift takedown of Morteza Ghiasi Cheka, pinned him down full stretch to score a victory by fall.

Going by the results of his earlier bouts, it was clear Bajrang would have a tough time in the semi-final against Haji Aliyev of Azerbaijan. Aliyev found his scoring zone in Bajrang's injured knee and stepped up the offensive with four takedowns. Aliyev led 8-1 as the time ticked away in the second and final period. Bajrang tried to make a comeback but Aliyev did not let the opportunity slip away, scripting a dominating 12-5 win.

It was most unfortunate that Bajrang had got injured a month before the Olympics as he had been preparing in a planned and thorough manner. From December 2020 till February 2021, Bajrang trained at the Cliff Kean Wrestling Club in Michigan. Not only were excellent sparring partners available but the gymnasium and the outdoor and training facilities were also very good. Then, Bajrang trained with his coach Shako Bentenidis at JSW'S Inspire Institute of Sport, Ballari, Karnataka. Finally, before the Olympics, Bajrang trained in Vladikavkaz, one of the main wrestling hubs in Russia that has produced many World and Olympic champions. The purpose of the training was to further improve Bajrang technically and help increase his concentration and functionality on the mat. Unfortunately, it all did not work out as expected.

Now something on Bajrang and his major achievements after he shifted to the freestyle 65 kg category. Bajrang began wrestling at the age of seven like most villagers in Haryana. His father who was a wrestler encouraged him to pursue the sport. His talent was spotted at Virender Kumar's akhada (wrestling pit) in 2005. Virender ji coached him till 2008. In 2008, Bajrang also trained with his idol Yogeshwar Dutt at the Chhatrasal Stadium in Delhi under the guidance of Ramphal ji and Satpal ji. In 2015, his family moved to Sonepat so that he could get quality coaching in the sport at the regional centre at the Sports Authority of India. After he moved into the freestyle 65 kg category, Bajrang has had quite a few notable successes. In May 2017, he won the gold medal in the Asian Wrestling Championships in New Delhi. In 2018, he won gold medals in his category in both the Gold Coast Commonwealth Games and the Asian Games. The same year, he won the silver medal in the World Championships in Budapest. In 2019, he won a bronze medal in the World Championships in Nur-Sultan, Kazakhstan and qualified for the Tokyo Olympics. He also won the 2020 Rome Ranking Series and the 2021 Matteo Pellicone Ranking Series held in Rome.

For his services to Wrestling, Bajrang Punia has been conferred by the Government of India the Arjuna Award in 2015 and the then Rajiv Gandhi Khel Ratna Award and the Padma Shri in 2019.

Neeraj Chopra – India's Second Individual Olympic Gold Medallist

On 7th August, Neeraj Chopra who was born on 24th December 1997 in Khandra, Haryana, became India's second individual Olympic gold medallist when he won the javelin throw event with a throw of 87.58 m in the Tokyo Olympics. Abhinav Bindra had won India's first individual Olympic gold in Shooting in the 2008 Beijing Olympics. Neeraj qualified for the final at Tokyo on 4th August by throwing 86.65 m - topping the javelin throw qualification round in the process.

In the final on 7th August, Neeraj, the thrower, was way ahead of his opponents. Neeraj settled any argument early with an effort of 87.58m in only his second try. The manner in which he approached the challenge helped in finishing off proceedings early. Strong and purposeful, Neeraj's quiet aggression and body language simply blew away the rest. It was a joy to behold.

Neeraj lives in a joint family in Khandra village, Panipat district, Haryana. He studied at DAV College, Chandigarh and joined the Indian Army at the rank of Naib Subedar in 2016. The javelin prodigy first hit the headlines when he became the under-20 javelin champion at the IAAF World under-20 Championships in Bydgoszcz, Poland in 2016. He set the junior world record. He also became the first Indian athlete to ever win a world title in Track and Field at the Under-20 level. The cut-off date for the 2016 Rio Olympics was 11th July otherwise Neeraj would have qualified for the Rio Olympics itself.

Apart from winning other golds, Neeraj won the gold medal in his event in both the 2018 Commonwealth Games and Asian Games. In May 2019, Neeraj underwent surgery of his throwing arm elbow which was performed by Dr Dinshaw Pardiwala at the Kokilaben Dhirubhai Ambani Hospital, Mumbai. He was out of action for nearly a year. In January 2020, Neeraj qualified for the 2020 Tokyo Olympics when he threw 87.86 m at the ACNE meeting in Potchefstroom, South Africa. Neeraj opened his international season of 2021 with a throw of 83.18 m that earned him the gold at an event in Lisbon, Portugal. **My interview with Neeraj follows:-**

How did you take to this sport?

For a while when small, I dreamt of becoming a cricketer but I was not too serious about it. I was a rather overweight kid - weighing 80 kg before I reached my teens. My uncle Bheem first took me to a nearby gymnasium and later on to the Shivaji Stadium in Panipat hoping that I would take up some sport. I used to observe athletes at the stadium. My senior Jaiveer, who had represented Haryana in javelin told me one day to try my hand at the sport instead of sitting doing nothing. I threw the javelin some 30-40 metres - a good distance for a novice. Jaiveer then took me under his wing and so my training in the sport began. My family got to know about my involvement in the sport only after my winning a competition was in the news.

Who were the other coaches who helped you and how?

Initially, it was Jaiveer who coached me. Kashinath Naik also helped me along the way. When I set the world junior record in 2016, I trained with the Australian coach Gary Calvert. Gary Calvert began the process of ironing out the faults in my technique. After that, the German coaches - Uwe Hohn and Dr Klaus Bartonietz - took over and played a great role in my Olympic success and overall improvement. I learnt so many new things from them. Both of them have great experience and deep knowledge about javelin throwing and I benefitted greatly from their inputs. They understood my body and made good training plans for me. Dr Klaus was with me when I won the Olympic gold.

What worked the most for you in the run-up to the Tokyo Olympics?

Without doubt, it was my participating in two or three international tournaments where the top throwers in the world including the ones who made it to the final in Tokyo took part. So, in the Olympics there was no pressure from the competitors on me. I needed to only focus on my throws.

What did Dr Klaus tell you before the Olympic final?

Dr Klaus told me to throw my best as early as possible. He told me not to leave anything to chance. An early good throw will put pressure on the other competitors. When I went into the final, I was mentally fresh with a clutter-free mind.

What were the thoughts going through your mind during the final?

When the final was underway, there was only one thought in my mind. The thought was that I had to give my best in all my throws. I was conscious that my body movement had to remain in sync with my throws as a slight deviation from technique could ruin an attempt. At the end, I realized that I had won the gold when the other competitors could not do as well as me even in their last attempts.

How is it that all the other competitors in the final seemed to be ' thrown' away by you in the Tokyo Olympics?

7th August, 2021 - the day of the final of the javelin throw event in the Tokyo Olympics was the greatest day of my life. I had prepared well for that day and by God's grace I was at my best. Other competitors complained about the surface being slippery and the weather being hot but I had only one target in mind - winning the gold. That was how, possibly, the others were 'thrown' away.

Finally, please suggest how India can win Olympic golds in other sports too.

For India to win Olympic golds in other sports, we need to develop a sports culture in our country. Proper selection of talent, training and competitive exposure must be provided from the grassroots level in all sports. Proper support is a must for all our sports persons at all stages so that they remain focussed. Again, for the next Olympics, special emphasis will have to be given to our potential medal winners at the 2024 Paris Games very soon.

Neeraj has the distinction of being the first Indian to win a gold on his Olympic debut. His silver medal at the 2022 World Championships made him the second Indian after Anju Bobby George to win a medal at a World Athletics Championships. He subsequently won the first gold for India at the 2023 World Athletics Championships at Budapest and his second Asian Games gold at the Hangzhou Asian Games.

For his services to Athletics, Neeraj was conferred the Arjuna Award in 2018, the Vishisht Seva Medal (VSM) in 2020, Major Dhyan Chand Khel Ratna Award in 2021, Param Vishisht Seva Medal in 2022 and Padma Shri in 2022. Both VSM and PVSM were for excellence in sports.

CHAPTER 20

NEERAJ CHOPRA'S SILVER AND MANU BHAKER'S DOUBLE BRONZE- BRIGHT SPOTS FOR INDIA AT PARIS

Neeraj Chopra's silver medal and shooter Manu Bhaker's two bronze medals were the bright spots of India's show at the Paris Olympics which were held from 26th July to 11th August 2024. Manu Bhaker's first medal was won in the 10m air pistol event while the other was won with Sarabjot Singh in the mixed team 10m air pistol event. India won three more bronze medals through shooter Swapnil Kusale in the men's 50m rifle three position event, the men's hockey team and wrestler Aman Sehrawat in the men's 57 kg category. At Paris, India got only six medals. whereas in Tokyo, it had won seven medals including a gold. **Neeraj Chopra's silver medal made him the first Indian to win a gold and a silver in successive Olympics. Manu Bhaker became the first Indian since independence to win two medals in one Olympic Games. Aman Sehrawat became the youngest Indian to win an Olympic medal at 21 years and 24 days. P V Sindhu had won her first Olympic medal at 21 years 1 month and 14 days in 2016.**

The Indian contingent for the Paris Games consisted of 110 athletes who competed in 16 sports. **For the Opening Ceremony, India's flag- bearers were P V Sindhu and Sharath Kamal - the table tennis player.**

Before going into detail about how India's medal winners won their medals at the Paris Olympics, I feel I need to mention the sad and unfortunate happening that resulted in wrestler Vinesh Phogat being disqualified from the 50kg wrestling event after becoming the first Indian woman wrestler to reach the final of an Olympic event. On

6th August, unseeded Vinesh Phogat, caused a huge upset by defeating top-seeded world and 2020 Tokyo Olympic champion Yui Susaki of Japan 3-2 in the round of 16. It is worth mentioning that Susaki had never lost an international match till this defeat. Vinesh then got the better of former European champion Oksana Livach of Ukraine 7-5 in the quarter-finals and the reigning Pan American Games champion Yusneylys Guzman 5-0 in the semi-finals to become the first Indian woman wrestler to reach the final of an Olympic event. Vinesh was to meet Sarah Ann Hildebrandt of USA in the final.

The next day, all Indian sports lovers were in for a shock. Despite the best efforts of the IOA officials and doctors, Vinesh's weight was found to be 100 grams in excess of the permitted 50 kg prior to the final - the second day weigh-in. This led to her sad disqualification after having achieved what no Indian woman wrestler had done before. Her appeal against her disqualification and for a joint silver medal as she had reached the final in the 50kg category was dismissed by the ad hoc division of the Court of Arbitration for Sport.

Manu Bhaker – First Indian Woman To Win Two Medals In One Olympic Games

Shooter Manu Bhaker got India's first medal at Paris - a bronze. It was the first Olympic medal to be won by a female Indian shooter. In fact, it was India's first Olympic medal in Shooting since the 2012 London Olympics.

Manu had participated in the 2020 Tokyo Olympics without

success despite being one of the best shooters in her events in the world. After her success in Paris, I asked Manu why she was much better in Paris than in Tokyo. Manu said, " At Tokyo, I was inexperienced for such a big stage, my preparation was not as good as it should have been and I was very nervous during matches being worried about the outcome. Stress got the better of me. In Paris, I was much better prepared with the coach's support and I was more mature and technically better having rectified the errors of the past."

At Tokyo, Manu achieved what no Indian athlete has done so far - winning two medals in one Olympic Games. On 27th July, Manu qualified for the final of the 10m air pistol event finishing third with a score of 580. In the final on the following day, Manu showcased her exceptional skill and composure, maintaining a top-three position for the majority of the event. She was 0.1 points ahead in second place heading into the final shot but ultimately slipped to third place to secure the bronze. She finished with 221.7 points.

On 29th July, Manu Bhaker and Sarabjot Singh qualified for the bronze medal match finishing third out of 17 pairs in the qualification round of the 10m mixed team air pistol event. As per the rules, the first two qualifiers played for the gold medal and the third and fourth qualifiers for the bronze. The following day, Manu and Sarabjot defeated South Korea's Oh Ye Jin and Wonho Li 16-10 to take the bronze medal. The Koreans took the first two points, but once Sarabjot settled down, the Indian pair took the next six points. The Koreans then recovered from

2-8 to make it 10-14. Oh Ye Jin, the Olympic champion struck 9 on her final shot while her partner managed 9.5. For India, Manu shot a 9.4 but a 10.2 from Sarabjot helped India win the bronze medal. In this event, Manu, in her second Olympics, exuded confidence from the start while Sarabjot, in his first Olympics, after some early nerves settled down to play really well. Earlier in the individual 10m pistol event, Sarabjot narrowly failed to qualify for the finals. Sarabjot did not let that loss affect him in the mixed team event that followed.

Manu's next event was the 25m air pistol. After finishing second in the qualifying round on 2nd August, with a score of 590, Manu made it to the final of the event. In the final on the following day, Manu was, for most part of the event, in the first four. For a brief while she was sixth. She shot extremely well in the sixth and seventh series but managed only two points in the following series to drop down. She had to play the fourth - place elimination round against Veronica Major of Hungary. In that match, Manu missed two targets and finished fourth while Veronica missed only one and took the bronze. "I do feel bad about narrowly missing out on a hat-trick of Olympic medals in the same Games but it is part and parcel of sports," said Manu.

Swapnil Kusale, who became India's first shooter to qualify for the men's 50m rifle 3 position Olympic final on 31st July, created history on the following day by becoming India's first Olympic medal winner in this category and that too, in his maiden Olympic appearance. Kusale was sixth after the kneeling event. However, some consistent shooting in the three series in the prone position and two series in standing positions, saw Kusale climb to the third position. Kusale continued to shoot consistently to maintain his third position and finish with a bronze. The win was a huge relief for Swapnil as he had agonizingly missed out on a medal at both the 2023 World Shooting Championships at Baku and the subsequent Asian Games in Hangzhou, China.

About how he won the Olympic bronze, Swapnil said, " I was very confident about my basic technique. During my entire match - qualification and finals, I only focused on my body and process not worrying about the result. During the qualification, I kept myself solution - oriented. Whatever problems I faced in one shot, I tried to find a solution before the next shot. Similarly in the finals, I also tried to focus on executing my technique correctly shot by shot."

Men's Hockey Side Finish With Bronze Again

At Paris, there were two pools comprising of six teams each. India was in Pool B alongwith Belgium, the defending champions, Argentina, Australia, Ireland and New Zealand. The top four teams of each pool qualified for the quarter - final stage.

The Indian hockey team led by star defender and drag-flicker Harmanpreet Singh won its second successive Olympic bronze medal at Paris when it defeated Spain 2-1 in the bronze medal play-off match on 8th August. The other outstanding player for India at Paris was goalkeeper P R Sreejesh who retired from international hockey at the end of the Paris Olympics. The team as a whole fought hard. **I asked both the captain Harmanpreet Singh, a three-time Olympian and Sreejesh, a four-time Olympian and captain of the Indian side at the 2016 Rio Olympics, a couple of questions each. I started with Sreejesh.**

Sreejesh, what points must a goalkeeper keep in mind so as to save penalty strokes in (a) before and after the 8-sec rule and (b) in the 8-sec rule ?

Before and after the 8-sec rule, one needs to believe more on one's instincts, analyze the player taking the stroke, his or her stance, grip and favourite angle. One needs to predict the ball's direction. In the 8-sec rule, the goalkeeper needs to think how to kill the 8 seconds. The goalkeeper must never commit himself or herself.

Of your two Olympic bronze medals, which is more special ?

The bronze medal we won in the 2020 Tokyo Olympics is closer to my heart, The Tokyo bronze was won after nearly four decades. That time we were not sure about winning a medal. It really meant a lot to all of us. This time at Paris, we were in the top six and capable of defeating any team. At Paris, we were expected to be among the top two which makes a laudable third place look a bit disappointing.

Harmanpreet, please share your thoughts on the team's performance at Paris.

We were unlucky to lose to Germany in the semi-final as we created several chances but getting back-to-back Olympic bronze medals is a huge achievement. Our players not only displayed skill, speed and coordination but also displayed the will to fight in difficult situations, never ever giving up. The quarter-final match against Great Britain was an example.

What has made you such an outstanding drag-flicker?

My being cool and utilizing my strengths in the best possible manner has helped me a lot. Bram Lomans, the brilliant Dutch drag-flicker gave me some useful tips. One must remember that drag-flicking is a simple process of scoring a goal. From the pusher to the teammates near the drag-flicker, all have an important part to play. With experience, I have found different ways of scoring. Strength-training is a must and we drag-flickers work a lot on the upper part of our body and back in the gym.

Indian Team : Standing (L to R) Gurjant Singh, Lalit Kumar Upadhyay, Amit Rohidas, Manpreet Singh, Mandeep Singh, Coach - Craig Fulton, Harmanpreet Singh (C), P. R. Sreejesh, Jarmanpreet Singh, Abhishek Nain.

Sitting (L to R) Sanjay Rana, Shamsher Singh, Hardik Singh, Krishan Bahadur Pathak, Sumit Walmiki, Nilakanta Sharma, Vivek Sagar Prasad, Sukhjeet Singh, Raj Kumar Pal, Jugraj Singh.

Note : Alternate players - Krishan Bahadur Pathak, Jugraj Singh, Nilakanta Sharma.

India began its hockey campaign at Paris by scoring a 3-2 win over New Zealand in a hard-fought Pool B on 27th July. The goalkeepers of both the sides produced a number of wonderful saves. New Zealand took the lead in the 8th minute through Sam Lane's powerful drag-flick. India then equalized through Mandeep Singh in the 24th minute and also went ahead in the 34th minute with Vivek Sagar Prasad scoring the goal. New Zealand then drew level in the 53rd minute when Simon Child scored a brilliant goal. Just as it seemed the match was heading for a draw, Harmanpreet Singh converted a penalty corner in the 59th minute to give India a win and three points.

In its second pool match against Argentina on 29th July, India secured a 1-1 draw. The match was evenly fought. Argentina took the lead in the 22nd minute through Lucas Martinez. In the 37th minute Argentina missed a golden opportunity of going ahead when Maico Casella failed to convert a penalty stroke. Skipper Harmanpreet Singh saved the day for India by converting a penalty corner in the 59th minute - a minute before the end.

India then defeated Ireland 2-0 in its third pool match on 30th July. India dominated the game for most of the time. Whenever Ireland attacked, they could not beat Sreejesh at goal. Skipper Harmanpreet Singh scored both the goals through penalty corners in the 11th and 19th minutes.

Belgium inflicted on India its first defeat on 1st August scoring a 2-1 win. India took the lead in the 18th minute when Abhishek Nain capitalized on a defensive error and smashed the ball low to the goalkeeper's right. Belgium's pressure was finally rewarded when Thibeau Stockbroekx scored in the 33rd minute to make the score 1-1. In the 44th minute,

Belgium took the lead through substitute John - John Dohmen. Belgium's defence remained unthreatened in the final quarter and the 2020 Olympic champions maintained the lead till the end of the game

In its final pool match on 2nd August, India scored a crucial 3-2 win over Australia. This was India's first victory against Australia in hockey at the Olympics since Munich 1972. As usual, goalkeeper Sreejesh brought off some brilliant saves. India took the lead in the 12th minute through Abhishek Nain and went two-up in the next minute when Harmanpreet Singh converted a penalty corner. Thomas Craig scored in the 25th minute to reduce India's lead. Just after half-time in the 32nd minute, Harmanpreet Singh converted a penalty stroke and India led 3-1. Five minutes before the final whistle, Blake Glovers converted a penalty stroke and the score read 3-2 in India's favour. The Indian defence saw out the remaining minutes without conceding another goal. India finished second in its pool.

India's quarter-final match against Great Britain on 4th August was evenly fought even though India played more than half the game with ten men – Amit Rohidas being shown a red card as his hockey stick hit William Calnan's face. Despite being down to 10 men, India never gave up. Harmanpreet converted a penalty corner in the 22nd minute with a superb drag-flick. Lee Morton equalized in the 27th minute and at half-time the score was 1-1. With the numerical advantage, Great Britain dominated the rest of the game but was unable to score till the end of the game as India put up a tight defence supported by the brilliant Sreejesh at goal. In the penalty shoot-out, Harmanpreet Singh, Sukhjeet

Singh, Lalit Kumar Upadhyay and Raj Kumar Pal scored for India while only James Albery and Zachary Wallace could score for Great Britain. India made it to the semi-finals by winning 4-2 in penalty shootout.

World champions Germany defeated India 3-2 in a hard-fought semi-final on 6th August. India missed the services of Amit Rohidas who was shown a red card in the quarter-final. India dominated the first quarter, taking an early lead when Harmanpreet Singh converted a penalty corner in the 7th minute. Germany scored twice in the second quarter to first equalize and then take the lead. Gonzalo Peillat drew level by converting a penalty corner in the 18th minute while Christopher Ruehr converted a penalty stroke in the 27th minute to put Germany in the lead. India drew level in the second half when Sukhjeet Singh deflected Harmanpreet Singh's penalty corner into the net in the 36th minute. In the 54th minute of play - with just six minutes to go, Marco Miltkau gave Germany the crucial lead by beating Sreejesh with a fine shot. India even replaced Sreejesh to bring in another attacker but to no avail. For the second successive Olympics, India failed to make it to the hockey final.

Despite conceding a goal in the 18th minute of play, India fought back to defeat Spain 2-1 on 8th August and clinch the hockey bronze medal for the second Olympics in succession. After the 1972 Munich Olympics, this is the first time the Indian hockey team has won medals in two successive Olympics. The first quarter ended goalless. In the 18th minute of the match, Spain took the lead when Marc Miralles converted a penalty stroke. India drew level in the last 14 seconds of the second quarter when skipper Harmanpreet Singh converted a penalty corner. Harmanpreet Singh converted another penalty corner in the 33rd minute to put India 2-1 ahead. Despite the match being well-contested, India protected its lead to win 2-1 and take the Olympic bronze medal again. Harmanpreet Singh with 10 goals finished as the top scorer of the tournament.

Results:

Pool B - beat New Zealand 3-2 (Mandeep Singh 1, Vivek Sagar Prasad 1, Harmanpreet Singh 1)

drew with Argentina 1-1 (Harmanpreet Singh 1)

beat Ireland 2-0 (Harmanpreet Singh 2)

lost to Belgium 1-2 (Abhishek Nain 1)

beat Australia 3-2 (Abhishek Nain 1, Harmanpreet Singh 2)

Quarter-final - beat Great Britain 1-1 (4-2 in the penalty shootout) (Harmanpreet Singh 1)

Semi-final - lost to Germany 2-3 (Harmanpreet Singh 1, Sukhjeet Singh 1)

Bronze medal play-off - beat Spain 2-1 (Harmanpreet Singh 2)

Final Positions - The Netherlands 1, Germany 2, India 3, Spain 4, Belgium 5, Australia 6, Great Britain 7, Argentina 8, South Africa 9, Ireland 10, France 11, New Zealand 12.

Neeraj Chopra – First Indian To Win Gold And Silver In Successive Olympics

Neeraj Chopra qualified on 6th August for the final of the javelin throw event on 8th August with a throw of 89.34m - the highest among all the qualifiers. Arshad Nadeem of Pakistan finished third with a throw of 86.59m. Neeraj was not at his best in the final with five of his throws being

declared foul. In his second throw - his only legal one - Neeraj threw 89.45m which was good enough to earn him the silver. When asked as to what went wrong, Neeraj said, " During the final, I couldn't push myself to the maximum. Mentally I was ready but I lacked physically. My leg work was not how it should have been. In this sport if your run up is not good or smooth, you cannot throw far. Injuries leading to Paris did affect me to an extent. Honestly, I have to work on being injury-free and on my technique as well." For the record, Neeraj became the first Indian sports person to win a gold medal and a silver in successive Olympics.

Pakistan's Arshad Nadeem, whose first throw was a foul like Neeraj, was at his best in his second throw. Nadeem's second throw was 92.97m, which not only broke the Olympic record but also earned him the gold medal. Nadeem's final throw was 91.79m.

AMAN SEHRAWAT – YOUNGEST INDIAN OLYMPIC MEDAL WINNER

On 9th August, Aman Sehrawat won a bronze medal in the 57 kg wrestling event to earn for India its sixth and last medal at the Paris Olympics. Aman, who is participating in his first Olympics, defeated Darian Cruz of Puerto Rico 13-5 in the bronze medal play - off. Aman became the youngest Indian to win an Olympic medal at 21years - 24 days.

Aman lost his parents early but being inspired by Sushil Kumar's silver medal in the 2012 London Olympics, he got enrolled at the Chhatrasal Stadium in North Delhi 10

years ago with the dream of becoming an Olympic medallist in the years to come. At Chhatrasal Stadium, Aman's life became more positive and purposeful. The coaches were there but it was his senior Sagar Phalswal, an experienced wrestler and a JWO in the Indian Air Force, who became his friend, philosopher and guide. He did everything possible to ensure that Aman would become a successful Olympian.

In 2022, at the age of 19, Aman won the gold medal at the Under - 23 World Championships at Pontevedra. After winning a bronze in the 57kg category at the 2022 Hangzhou Asian Games, Aman won the gold medal in the 2023 Asian Wrestling Championships in Astana. To make it to Paris, Aman defeated Ravi Dahiya, the 2020 Tokyo Olympics silver medallist in the 57 kg category selection trials. Before going to the Paris Olympics, Aman had rigorous practice in Russia.

I asked Aman to tell us about his bouts at the Paris Olympics. This is how Aman described his bouts. "On 8th August, I won the round of 16 very comfortably against Vladimir Egorov of Macedonia by virtue of technical superiority. In the next round, I had to face Albania's Chechen wrestler Zelimkhan Abakarov. Abakarov had beaten me 10-0 at the World Championships. I realized that I had to defeat him if I wanted to win a medal. Against Abakarov, I decided not to give him any points at the start so that I could keep the contest as close as possible. I was ready for a long bout. The plan worked and I won 12-0. In the semi-final, I was pitted against Japan's Rei Higuchi. Against the Japanese, I lost four early points. Trying to cover up the deficit, I hurried and as a result I lost 0-10 via technical superiority inside two minutes. For the bronze medal bout the following day, I decided to be free and relaxed, just focusing on my game and bout. The result was I defeated Puerto Rico's Darian Cruz 13-5 to win the bronze.

Of the seven medal winners at the Tokyo Olympics, only Neeraj Chopra and the hockey team won medals at Paris. Wrestlers Bajrang Punia and Ravi Dahiya did not qualify. Weightlifter Saikhom Mirabai Chanu finished fourth while P.V. Sindhu and boxer Lovlina Borgohain lost early.

CHAPTER 21
SOME INTERESTING DETAILS ABOUT INDIAN OLYMPIC MEDAL WINNERS

1. (a) First person to win two medals in the same Olympics - Norman Pritchard (Athletics) - two silvers in 1900.

   (b) First woman to achieve this feat - Manu Bhaker (Shooting) - two bronze in 2024.

2. First person to win an individual gold in an Olympics - Abhinav Bindra (Shooting) in 2008.

3. First person to win gold and silver in successive Olympics- Neeraj Chopra (Athletics) - gold in 2020, silver in 2024.

4. (a) First person to win medals in successive Olympics - Sushil Kumar (Wrestling) bronze in 2008 and silver in 2012.

   (b) First woman to achieve this feat - P. V. Sindhu (Badminton) - silver in 2016 and bronze in 2020.

5. Only player to date to have represented India in 7 Olympics - Leander Paes (Tennis) - 1992, 96 - bronze, 2000, 04, 08, 12 and 16.

6. Players to have represented India in 4 Olympics with medals in each one of them - Leslie Walter Claudius (Hockey) - 1948 - gold, 1952- gold. 1956 - gold and 1960 - silver as captain and Udham Singh Kullar (Hockey) - 1952 - gold, 1956 - gold, 1960 - silver and 1964 - gold

7. Three Olympians from one family - Dhyan Chand (1928, '32 and '36 as captain), his brother Roop Singh (1932 and '36) and his son Ashok Kumar (1972 and '76) and

Harmik Singh (1968 and '72 as captain), his brother Ajit Singh (1972 and '76) and his nephew Gagan Ajit Singh (2000 and '04)

8. Father and son as Olympians - Dhyan Chand (1928, '32, '36) and Ashok Kumar(1972, '76), Ahmed Sher Khan (1936) and Aslam Sher Khan (1972), Vece Paes (Hockey in 1972)and Leander Paes (Tennis 1992 - 2016) and Ajit Singh(1972, '76) and Gagan Ajit Singh (2000, '04).

9. Brothers as Olympians - Dhyan Chand (1928, '32, '36 and Roop Singh (1932, '36), V J Peter (1960, '64 and '68) and V J Phillips (!972, '76), Balbir Singh Grewal and Gurbaksh Singh Grewal (both 1968) and Harmik Singh and Ajit Singh (1972)

10. Medal-winning players and coaches of medal-winning teams - Kishan Lal - 1948 captain and 1960 coach , Dharam Singh (Sr) - 1952 player and 1964 coach, Balkishan Singh - 1956 player and 1968 and 1980 coach and K D Singh 'Babu' - 1952 captain and 1972 coach.

11. Joint Captains - Prithipal Singh and Gurbux Singh in the 1968 Mexico Olympics where India got the bronze for the first time.

12. Olympian who won a Vir Chakra - Haripal Kaushik (1956 gold, 1960 silver and 1964 gold) won it in the 1962 Chinese war.

13. Only Indian hockey Olympian to play with spectacles - Gurbux Singh- 1964 gold and 1968 bronze as joint captain.

14. Not conceding a goal in Olympic Hockey - India in 1928 at Amsterdam and 1956 at Melbourne.

15. The four Balbir Singhs - The great Balbir Singh (Sr) / Balbir Singh Dosanjh - centre - forward (1948, '52 and '56 as captain). Balbir Singh Kullar - a forward (Punjab)- 1964 and '68 Olympian, Balbir Singh Kullar - a half-back (Services) -1968 Olympian and Balbir Singh Grewal - forward (Railways) - 1968 Olympian.

(L to R) - Balbir (Punjab), Balbir (Sr), Balbir (Services), Balbir (Rlys).

16. Three-time Olympian Ajitpal Singh (bronze in 1968, '72 and captain in 1976) has the distinction of captaining the only Indian hockey team to win the World Cup in 1975 at Kuala Lumpur.

SOME MORE INFORMATION RELATING TO HOCKEY

1. Pargat Singh is the only hockey player to captain India in two Olympics - 1992 and 1996. India did not win a hockey medal.

2. Harmanpreet Singh (2020) is the fourth Indian Olympian to lead India to victory in the Asian Games at Hangzhou. The three earlier successful Indian captains at the Asian Games were Shankar Laxman in 1966, Dhanraj Pillay in 1998 – both at Bangkok and Sardara or Sardar Singh in 2014 at Incheon.

3. Three-time Olympian Harmanpreet Singh is the only medal - winning Olympic captain (2024) to have led an Asian Games winning team (2022).

4. Harbail Singh is the only non-Olympian to coach two Olympic gold medal winning hockey teams-1952 and 1956.

5. The great Ashwini Kumar - a versatile genius who headed the Indian Hockey Federation- had the rare privilege of witnessing and being part of 17 Summer Olympics from London 1948 till London 2012 (both included), a record that will be hard to beat.

6. Australia's Graham Reid, the chief coach of the 2020 Tokyo Olympics bronze medal winning Indian men's hockey side, is the first foreign hockey coach to achieve this feat with an Indian team.

7. Craig Fulton of Great Britain, is the second foreign chief coach to help India win an Olympic medal- bronze at the 2024 Paris Olympics.

CHAPTER - 22
INDIA'S AGONIZING FOURTH-PLACE FINISHES AT THE OLYMPICS

1. **Randhir Shinde** – Men's 54kg Freestyle Wrestling - 1920 Antwerp Olympics.

2. **Keshav Mangave** – Men's 62kg Freestyle Wrestling- 1952 Helsinki Olympics.

3. **Team India** – Football – 1956 Melbourne Olympics.

4. **Milkha Singh** – Men's 400m, Athletics – 1960 Rome Olympics.

5. **Prem Premnath** – Men's 57kg Freestyle Wrestling - 1972 Munich Olympics.

6. **Sudesh Kumar** – Men's 52 kg Freestyle Wrestling – 1972 Munich Olympics.

7. **Women's hockey** – 1980 Moscow Olympics.

8. **P T Usha** – Women's 400m Hurdles, Athletics - 1984 Los Angeles Olympics.

9. **Rajinder Singh** – Men's 74kg Freestyle Wrestling - 1984 Los Angeles Olympics.

10. **Leander Paes-Mahesh Bhupati** – Men's Doubles in Tennis - 2004Athens Olympics

11. **Kunjarani Devi** – Women's 48kg Weightlifting - 2004 Athens Olympics.

12. **Joydeep Karmakar** – Men's 50m Rifle Prone Shooting - 2012 London Olympics.

13. **Abhinav Bindra** – Men's 10m Air Rifle Shooting – 2016 Rio Olympics.

14. **Sania Mirza – Rohan Bopanna** – Mixed Doubles in Tennis - 2016 Rio Olympics.

15. **Dipa Karmakar** – Women's Vault, Gymnastics – 2016 Rio Olympics.

16. **Aditi Ashok** – Women's Golf – 2020 Tokyo Olympics.

17. **Women's Hockey Team** – 2020 Tokyo Olympics.

18. **Deepak Punia** – Men's Wrestling 86 kg – 2020 Tokyo Olympics.

19. **Arjun Babuta** – Men's 10m Air Rifle Shooting – 2024 Paris Olympics

20. **Dhiraj Bommadevara – Ankita Bhakat** – Mixed Team Archery – 2024 Paris Olympics.

21. **Manu Bhaker** – Women's 25m Air Pistol Shooting– 2024 Paris Olympics.

22. **Maheshwari Chauhan – Anant Jeet Singh Naruka** – Mixed Team Skeet Shooting – 2024 Paris Olympics.

23. **Lakhsya Sen** – Men's Badminton Singles – 2024 Paris Olympics.

24. **Saikhom Mirabai Chanu** – Women's Weightlifting 49 kg – 2024 Paris Olympics.